VW Camper – The Inside Story

A Guide to VW Camping Conversions and Interiors 1951–2005

David Eccles

The Crowood Press

First published in 2005 by
The Crowood Press Ltd
Ramsbury, Marlborough
Wiltshire SN8 2HR

www.crowood.com

This impression 2008

British Library Cataloguing-in-Publication Data
A catalogue record for this book is available from the British Library.

ISBN 978 1 86126 763 4

Some words, model names and designations are trademarked and are the property of the trademark holder. They have been used for identification purposes only and this is not an official publication.

Whilst every effort has been made to ensure the accuracy of all material, the author and publisher cannot accept liability for loss resulting from any error, mis-statement, inaccuracy or omission contained herein. The author welcomes any corrections or additional information.

This book has been compiled with the help and support of the VW Bus community all over the world. Many individuals have lent brochures, taken pictures, provided information and photographs, carried out research or provided contacts, and without their knowledge and enthusiasm this book would not have been possible. In particular I should like to thank:

Michael Steinke Archives, Andreas Plogmaker Archives, Steve Saunders Archives, Lind Bjornsen Archives, Heino Vanska Archives, Rob Kneisler, Jens Zeemans, Geoff Lucas, Malcolm Bobbit, Richard Stainsby, Duncan Fagg, Tom Brouillette, Allan Ward, Paul Price, Justin Warden, Norman Benkert, John Christmas, Thomas Gahl, Paul Trafford, Dave Cantle, Simon Holloway, Nigel Skeet, Barry Carpenter, Peter Cage, Mike Howles, David Gander, Marion Roberts aka Issy, Alan Malone, Glenn Robbins, Jon aka Madmaveric, Tim Lees, Mike Howles, Richard Folks, Neil Smart, Jamie Dorsett, Glenn Robbins, Paul Norbury.

Thanks also to Volkswagen AG, Auto-Sleeper, Bilbo's, Devon, Danbury Motor Caravans, Deepcar Motorhomes Ltd, VW Camper and Commercial magazine, The Split Screen Van Club, The Type 2 Owner's Club, Club 80–90 and NEATO for their help and support.

Photography by David Eccles except for:
Vince Molenaar (Amescador), Bill Moore (Australian 58), Graham Darlington (Australian 59), Ade Pitkin (Australian Adventurer), Diana Anderson (Syncro Adventurewagen), Larry Edson (71 Adventurewagen), Joe Federici (T25 Adventurewagen), Ralph Pettit (Westfalia T4), Alex Muir (Bilbo), Jim Taylor (Canadiana), Ian Frampton (68 Canterbury Pitt), Tony Hammond (Danbury), Colin Mew (67 Danbury), Mark Walker (72 Danbury and Devonette), Brian Ford (63 Dormobile), Glen Taylor (72 Dormobile), Ben Hayes (67 SA Camper, 80 Moonraker), Kavan O'Connell (Holdsworth), John Stanton (EZ), Taylor Nelson (67 Riviera), William Meyer (75 Riviera), Von and Shaun (Viking), Tonny Larsen (50 Poba), Stuart McQuarrie (60 Poba), Stephen Aylott (T3 Eurovette), David Pickles (85 Holdsworth), John (Sunderland, Devon Torvette), Kevin Jackson (Devon Torvette), Graham Booth (72 Caravette), Lawrence Gibbons (78 Moonraker), Ken Hathaway (72 Moonraker), Scott Doering (SO 23), Thom Fitzpatrick (55 Westy), Joe Crocket (SO 34), Mark Merz (62 Westy), Kevin Brown (78 Helsinki), Stan Wohlfarth (81 Westy), George Deverick (81 Joker), Torsten Stoll (Safaré), Steve Nolan (58 Westy and 67 Arcomobil), Beetles UK (Danbury Rio/Surf).

I should also like to thank any owner, not mentioned above, whose Camper and interior are shown herein, and also those who took the time and trouble to arrange for me to photograph their Camper. If I have inadvertently omitted to mention anyone or credit any photographs please let me know for any future edition.

This book is dedicated to my wife, Cee.

Typeset by Alex Ellis

Printed and bound in Singapore by Craft Print International.

Contents

Since its introduction in March 1950, the Volkswagen Transporter and Microbus has become an instantly recognizable, classic icon on roads all over the world. Of all its uses, special bodies and variants, the VW Campervan is the most popular and best known, and the VW Camper, in its many different forms, is what is documented and celebrated inside this book.

The book aims to describe and illustrate the various different models and interior layouts used by the professional conversion companies which converted VW Buses into Campers. No book could definitively document every single conversion built over the past fifty five years, but this book includes all the main models and conversions produced in the UK, Europe and North America, as well as many lesser known and unusual conversions from other parts of the world. For ease of reference the conversions have been listed in alphabetical order, and, wherever possible, all generations of the VW produced by a company have been described in chronological order within that chapter.

From this book it should be possible not only to identify what make and model a particular Camper is, but also to see what would have been originally fitted in the van. A word of caution, however – things are not always what they seem. Sometimes firms would produce prototypes for advertising purposes, and fitments would occasionally change from those illustrated in brochures. Additionally, many items were optional extras, so what may appear to be a standard fitting may actually be an extra. Couple this with the fact that a customer could also specify addition of units or items from a higher-in-the-range model, or delete items from a standard model, and the notion that all Campers of a particular model and year are necessarily identical becomes questionable. For example, one of the Buses in the book shows an interior with tables that were used for an earlier year, but the customer could not stand the bright orange finish so requested they were changed. This is only known because the original owner still has that interior, but now has it fitted to an earlier Bus! Then, of course, there is retro fitting, whereby furniture or items from one year or model have at some point been fitted into a different model or year, so you can have a Devon Caravette with a Richard Holdsworth Roof, or a 1978 Moonraker interior fitted to a 1976 Bus, thus appearing to be an original 1976 Moonraker even though the model was not introduced until 1978! Then there is the fact that items get lost or removed over time, and also that various owners may have carried out updates and modifications to suit themselves …

The table in this 1972 Devon interior should be orange to match the sink worktop, but the customer who bought it new decided she could not stand the orange so asked Devon to substitute it!

In 1967 the only style of elevating roof available from Devon conversions was the Dormobile version. When the Bay Window model was introduced in 1968, with Devon's own new style of pop-top roof, the owner of this 1967 Split immediately took his Camper to Devon to have the new style of roof fitted.

However, as far as possible, the specifications and interior layouts described for each model here have been verified by both sales literature and period motoring press articles, and by tracking down surviving examples. So, not only should it be possible to determine what would have been the standard furniture and equipment supplied with a particular model, but also to see what other models in the range consisted of and what options were available for each model. Although there are several basic layouts for the 'box on wheels' Camper, each conversion has its own distinctive characteristics, and its own loyal supporters.

Before 1939 motorhomes and motor caravans were heavy, coach-built affairs, and the province of the well-off. The arrival of the VW Bus in 1950 came when Europe was rebuilding itself after the ravages of war, and at the start of a period of rising prosperity coupled with more leisure time. The Kombi model in

particular, with its removable bench seating, proved especially popular because of its unique ability to double as commercial load hauler in the week and family leisure vehicle at weekends. Here at last was an affordable vehicle that could be used for work and play.

Advertising brochures over the past fifty years provide a fascinating glimpse into changing lifestyles and fashions, as well as consumer expectations and ambitions, but one thing endures – owning a Campervan provides the freedom to go where and when you please and to get away from the hurly burly of daily life. Living with a VW Bus in particular is more about lifestyle than with any other marque, and although the media perpetuate the myth that VW Campers were owned by flower-waving hippies, the truth is they were, and are, owned by people of all ages and generations, from all sorts of backgrounds and with diverse attitudes and aspirations. There is,

however, something special about a VW Camper, and no matter where you travel in it, your Bus will always be a subject of interest and conversation.

1951–67
T1: SPLIT SCREEN CAMPERS

It was Westfalia, back in 1951, who introduced the world to the VW Camper. Their early Camping Boxes were just that, self-contained units that had all the essentials needed to camp in a Bus, and which simply lifted in or out of the vehicle. Their early advertising even highlighted the option of using the Camping Box equipment in the home for houseguests! Other cabinets, such as a toiletry cabinet on the load door, were optional add-ons. By 1955 Westfalia were producing fully fitted Campers and the introduction of SO 23 in 1959 set the standard for others to follow.

In the UK, motorhomes were fast gaining in popularity, but import duties meant many well-established

This 1971 Devon has a long elevating roof, something not available from Devon at that time. In fact, it is a Holdsworth roof, fitted for a subsequent owner.

converters used vehicles other than the Volkswagen. Dormobile were among the first UK converters of motor caravans, and their patent elevating roof was available on their models well before the VW received a version. Peter Pitt was the first person in the UK to convert a VW Bus into a Camper, in 1956. Because of the higher price of imported VWs, the Pitt Moto-Caravan conversion was mainly based on UK marques such as the Austin, and full-scale production of his conversions on the VW base did not really get under way until 1960. However, his open-plan arrangement, developed in 1956 and allowing for dinette style eating and a flexible furniture arrangement, influenced Campervan design for those who were to follow.

Devon showed their first VW conversions in 1957, followed by Moortown in 1958 and the European Cars Slumberwagen in 1959. The VW Dormobile did not make an appearance until 1961, and Danbury versions were available from 1964. During the 1960s only Devon, Dormobile and Danbury (and Westfalia of course) were officially sanctioned by VW; other conversions had to offer their own warranty. In Europe and North America the Westfalia ruled supreme but, during the 1960s, demand for Westfalia Campers in the US far outstripped supply, giving rise to a series of US Campers such as EZ, Sundial and Road Runner, all closely modelled on Westfalia designs and layouts.

1960: Elevating Roofs Arrive

Although the Dormobile elevating roof had been fitted to vehicles from 1957, it was not until 1960 that the VW Bus had an elevating roof available as a fitted option, with European Cars offering the unique Calthorp elevating roof. The German converter Arcomobil also offered an elevating roof from 1961, but instead of cutting the roof they used factory sunroof models direct from VW, minus the sliding gear and canvas. In 1962 Devon offered its own Gentlux elevating roof, but the

newly introduced VW Dormobile had already broken new ground and, by 1963, Devon were offering the Dormobile roof as an option instead of their own version. Although Westfalia had an opening roof hatch for their conversions almost from the beginning, it was not until 1964 that Westfalia also offered elevating roofs, either their own pop-top version or a version featuring the Martin Walter Dormobile roof.

1968–79
T2: BAY WINDOW CAMPERS

By the time of the introduction of the new generation of Transporter in August 1967, with the curved one-piece 'Bay' windscreen and roomier interior, the VW Campervan was one of the best-known and most popular camping conversions, with elevating roofs becoming the norm along with pull-out (rock-and-roll) beds, which replaced the tiresome laying out of boards. Devon and Danbury had their own pop-top roofs, and Westfalia introduced a new style of elevating roof, hinged at the front, with an integral roof rack at the rear. In 1972 this Westfalia roof changed to being hinged at the rear, with the integral roof rack over the front cab. Holdsworth began converting VWs into Campers in 1967, and their Bay models featured an aluminium-sided elevating roof. All elevating roof models had the option of hammock bunks, but the Viking Spacemaker roof, introduced in 1974, created a huge space for sleeping. Fixed high tops, with full width upper berths, also began to be popular, with firms like Sheldon offering high tops and a fitting service, rather than a complete camping conversion.

The early 1970s saw an end to the solid wood interiors for most conversions, although there seemed to be a passion for orange, browns and beiges! The new melamine and laminate surfaces, often still in wood-look, were cheaper, lighter and thought to be more modern looking. In reality, something was lost in build quality, with the craftsman wood-

working being replaced by mass production of easily assembled units.

1980–90:
THE T3 (T25)

The third generation of VW Bus (often known as the T25 instead of T3) marked a significant change in terms of luxury and fitments. It was a very different vehicle from the previous slow workhorses, more spacious and better equipped and designed as a vehicle for the 1980s, bringing together advances in design, engineering and styling. Camping interiors reflected this, with comfort and style leading the design. Items such as sinks, gas/electric fridges and mains hook-up were now essential equipment rather than optional extras. Interior trim and fitments were more luxurious, with swivelling front seats often being standard, giving more flexibility. Interior layouts and fittings began to resemble luxury caravans or recreational vehicles (RVs). Furniture and cabinet work used modern laminates and pastel colours, with co-ordinated fabrics and fittings.

1990–2002:
THE T4

The production of sophisticated motor caravans continued into the T4 and, from 2004, the T5 platforms. Interiors were often better equipped and furnished than many homes, with microwaves, ovens, showers, satellite navigation, television, and CD/DVD players forming just part of the picture – a world away from the Camping Box or beds that were made up by laying down boards and tables and rearranging the seat cushions! There is, however, a predictable sameness about the modern conversions and maybe something has been lost along the way – part of the appeal of the early Campers was the simple approach to life, where one could just bundle children or friends into the Bus, throw in the bedding, hit the road and grab the chance to swap one lifestyle for another, leaving the clutter of daily life behind.

This 1951 'Barndoor Bus' is one of the first, if not the first, professional, fully fitted camping conversions, and pre-dates Westfalia's first fully fitted Camper by just a couple of months. It is certainly the oldest original condition VW Camper to survive, and, as such, is a piece of living history, as it is still used today, instead of residing in a museum.

Built in May 1951, on chassis number 20-13280, it was delivered to a car dealer in Dresden, East Germany, with no interior seating but with windows fitted. The dealer then had a professional Dresden Karosserie (coach-builder) convert it into a Camper in early 1952. The fitted original roof rack is similar to the very first Westfalia ones, in that it is bolted directly onto the roof using the internal bracing struts. The interior was well appointed and luxurious for its time, consisting of three wooden box units to form a U shape, much like the early Poba kits (see Chapter 23). The bench seat behind the bulkhead hinges up to reveal a built-in sink and two-burner cooker, and, at one end, is a section specifically designed to

house the gas bottle. The sink has a waste-water outlet but no tap or pump. The rear bench seat also houses the fitted petrol heater and its controls. There is a storage unit above the engine compartment and a sleeping mattress lays on a board above the engine to form a roomy child's bed. The cabinet work is well-crafted in solid oak. The upholstery is believed to be the original fabric, with PVC edges; though a little worn, it is still in good condition. The seat back cushions are mounted on boards, which simply lay between the front and rear units to make up the bed. Matching fabric panels have been applied to the side walls and load doors, with a matching roof border trim. Headliner has been fitted and there is an opening roof light, also with matching fabric trim, and a circular roof interior light. The curtains are all mounted on metal rods, one for each window. In 1952 this was camping in style!

Over the next nine or ten years the Bus was used as a Campervan and during this time the vehicle changed hands twice. The third owner was a fire

chief in a small village outside Dresden. He acquired the vehicle in 1962 and used the Bus as his personal transport and as a Camper, but he also used it for work. The Bus was used to haul a Volkswagen-powered water fire pump on a trailer to fires in the surrounding areas and also doubled as carrier for the fire crew.

The fire department used the vehicle for the next twenty-five years, until the death of the fire chief in 1987. His widow donated the Bus to the local fire service museum, where it was displayed for the next fifteen years until it was put up for sale to make way for another fire truck exhibit. Maurice Klok, from Classic VW specialists Kieft en Klok, acquired the Bus in 2002 and upon getting the vehicle back to Holland he simply put engine oil in (previously it was dry), filled it up with petrol, connected a new battery and the Bus fired up first time after standing for fifteen years!

In September 2002 Richard Burrows bought the Bus from Kieft en Klok and it arrived at Harwich docks, in England, on 30 September 2002. In the first two years after acquiring the Bus, Richard and his family covered over 5,000 miles (8,000km), including a trip to Bad Camberg 2003 and a two-week tour of Holland and Germany, which took in a visit to the Bus's birthplace in Wolfsburg. He has found the interior to be both practical and comfortable, although the old East German cooker has had to be upgraded, as the East German fittings and connections were not compatible with European Standards. He has also replaced the slow 25hp engine with a later 1300cc Beetle unit. Apart from that, everything, including the gearbox, is original and Richard plans to keep the Bus running for as long as possible before having to do any restoration work. Forty-three years on, this VW Camper is still doing exactly what it was designed for – giving a family the freedom to travel and camp in comfort.

Cushioning has vinyl edges – a very modern touch. Storage lockers for kitchen and toiletry equipment are sited in the front bench.

The opening roof light has matching trim, but obviously is not watertight!

The seat lifts up to reveal a washing bowl and cooker; the original East German cooker did not comply with EU fittings and regulations and has been replaced.

A petrol heater is sited in the rear bench unit; the original heater controls and heat outlet are on its end panel.

Travel/living mode. Everything stores neatly in the simple three-storage-box seat arrangement.

The nickname 'Barndoor Bus' is because of the very large engine lid fitted on pre-March 1955 models. Note the flashers discreetly added to the bumpers for extra safety on modern roads. The roof rack is attached directly onto the roof.

Seat cushions lay out to form a roomy double bed.

Back in 1963 a young couple, Ed and Jereen Anderson from California, decided to get out and see the world. They wanted the freedom to travel where and when they chose, and decided that a VW Bus was the ideal vehicle for this. Not liking the conversions around at the time, and wanting something that would be self-contained for travelling off the beaten track, they decided to build their own!

And so, in the carport of a motel in Coventry, England, plans took shape and the first Adventurer was born and actually built! They did not want a pop-top roof as these did not give any storage space, nor did they like the typical bed arrangements of the time, which were multi-cushioned sleeping platforms rather than beds. Additionally, many conversions used portable cookers and cool boxes and they wanted a proper cooker and a fridge.

What the Andersons came up with, and built, incorporated a rigid permanent high roof section, a one-piece mattress bed that could be folded away 'made up', a built-in propane cooker and fridge, gravity-fed water for a sink unit with drain, a toilet and ample storage.

They spent the next seventeen months travelling in their Adventurer, taking in thirty-one countries and

four continents, and covering 40,000 miles (64,360km) in the process. A real Adventure! Apparently Ed had the idea for starting a VW conversion business whilst in the middle of the Sahara Desert, as their Camper was proving ideal, especially for places with no campsites and facilities.

On their return to California in 1965, Ed set about turning his dream into reality and began to build Adventurers, using what had been learned from living in a van for a year and a half. Although some conversions were made on Split Buses as one-off orders, the business did not really get going until 1968 with conversions based on the new generation of Buses. This was a serious Camper, designed and built from experience, using an innovative, streamlined, fibre-glass top. It is still possible to get really remote in the US even today, and the Adventurewagen was designed specifically to give people the freedom to explore the wilderness, whilst being self-contained and comfortable. Initially, conversions were carried out in the Andersons' three-car garage, but soon they expanded into larger premises. By 1971, Adventure Campers Inc. had achieved state-wide distribution through VW dealerships.

However, by 1972 Ed felt the business was getting too big and was unhappy with the way quality was being compromised by high volume sales, so he sold the company and moved to Fort Bragg on the Mendocino coast in California. Just eighteen months later the company he left behind had mismanaged itself into bankruptcy, and so, in 1974, Ed set himself up in business again, now trading as Adventurewagen. He stayed put in Fort Bragg and concentrated on producing limited editions, focusing on quality and design. Between 1974 and 1979 he produced what many feel is the ultimate VW Camper. Sales were largely based on word of mouth from satisfied customers, and, by the time of the introduction of the new T25 (known as the Vanagon in the US) in 1980, Ed had built several hundred Adventure-wagens. Although brochures were produced, many Adventurewagens were built to order and tailored to meet specific requirements. Vanagons were used throughout the eighties, but, with the introduction of the T4 in 1990, Ed concentrated on converting Fords. Finally, around 2003/4, he carried out his last conversion (on a Ford, for himself) before finally shutting up shop and enjoying retirement!

The example featured here is a 1971 Adventurer owned by Larry Edson. The fibreglass roof with sliding window and integral rear roof rack and storage areas is the most obvious feature of an Adventurewagen.

Hot water on tap was a very advanced feature for the time. Note the marbled table and worktops for that luxury kitchen feel.

THE ADVENTURER

The Adventurer conversion featured fittings normally found only in luxury motorhomes. Water was pressurized and a mains water hook-up was standard (well ahead of the Camp-mobiles, which did not have this until the mid seventies). An Everpure water purification system meant that water was always fresh and safe. A special stainless steel container even delivered gravity-fed hot water at the sink! The built-in propane cooker had a gas tank that would last for six weeks and the electric fridge had a cross top freezer as standard. To run this efficiently, a special heavy duty Trojan air-cooled battery system was installed, consisting of six separate cell modules to provide 150 AH at 12V. Between the front seats was a portable seat with built-in toilet, and a snack table could be fitted in the front cab.

The roof is one of the most distinctive features of an Adventure-wagen, providing a standing height of 6ft (1.8m) with two large, screened awning style windows (which could be left open on rainy days), a wind-adjusted roof vent, with built-in 12V reversible fan, and two extra interior lights. On each side of the roof at the rear were hollow fins for storing fishing rods and gear, with a built-in roof rack between them.

Westfalia influences can be seen in the cooker/cool box unit with side-attached folding table.

The high roof provides ample storage both front and rear.

Around 1973 a new design full length version of the roof became available to order, with a distinctive 'whale tail' profile at the rear and an inset small rear window.

THE ADVENTURER VII

The new T25 was known as the Vanagon in the US, taking the name from VAN and station wAGON. Ed Anderson's claim was 'Adventurewagen's ultimate goal is to produce, without compromise, the finest possible Vanagon conversion'. The conversion was not marketed through the VW dealerships, which enabled it to be very cost-effective, and customers were even encouraged to bring their new Vanagon to Adventurewagen for conversion. The roof was now full length and featured a rear window in the 'whale tail'. Production was quite limited, with the emphasis on build and design quality and, so sure of the quality, customers were actively encouraged to compare the conversion with the Westfalia! Brochures advertising the new Adventurewagen even compared specifications point by point.

The Vanagon version certainly was luxurious and well equipped. The interior was built of hardwood, using cherry, teak, black walnut or oak, whereas 'like most products today the Westfalia is basically made of plastic'.

Storage space consisted of a wardrobe, shelves, spice rack, notions cabinet, hampers and storage for canned goods, fishing rods, suitcases, utensils and dishes. Privacy curtains screened top, bottom and cab, and flooring was wipe-clean vinyl. When comparing with the Westy the point was made that 'Experienced RVers who have had unremovable carpet in their first Camper rarely want it again.' The front passenger swivel seat was standard and differed from the Westy only in that it had access to a special high-intensity reading light. A propane heater was standard and solar panels provided water heating. It was even possible to arrange a camp shower set-up.

The fresh water supply kept the innovative design from 1968 of not using any plastic because of the 'objectionable taste that plastic imparts to water and because plastic water tanks eventually crack and leak'. Water was carried in an air-pressurized aluminium tank. In addition, the Everpure filtration system ensured water could be safe (or made safe if quality was questionable), as well as taste fresh. Water supply to the sink

also had adjustable flow and there was a 13gal (59ltr) holding tank for waste water when campsite hook-up was unavailable.

Given the popularity in the US of large motorhomes, or recreational vehicles (RV), that featured every home comfort imaginable, the Adventurewagen packed all those features into a small vehicle, which could get to places the large motor-homes could not manage. This, combined with a build quality not based on mass production, is what makes the Adventurewagen a bit special and certainly not just another OTW (Other Than Westfalia)! Advertising from the 1970s sums up this unique conversion:

Based on extensive personal experience, the Adventure Camper is geared to meet the special needs of travel and camping enthusiasts. Every day, people looking for compact, portable homes that really are compact and portable, come to Adventure. Adventurers looking toward Alaska, Latin America, Europe and all across the United States seek what the Andersons created – an economical and convenient way of living while travelling. And they find what they need.

A 1990 Adventurewagen on a Syncro base.

The neat Adventurewagen logo is also built into the front overhead cabinet.

This 1970s brochure depicts all three layouts and the three roof options as well as the optional tent awning.

The Dutch company Ames had been involved in the motor trade since 1905, and in 1947 became one of the first VW importers in Holland. As well as sales, they also had a commercial vehicle works where they made bodies and interiors to customer requirements. When people began trading-in their Split Screen VW models for the new Bay Window models and demand for Westfalia Campers began to rise, Ames decided it was cheaper and easier to convert Campers themselves rather than to import the expensive Westfalia versions. Westfalia Campers in Holland carried a massive 35 per cent import tax, but commercial vehicles were exempt. Thus a Panel van or Kombi could be imported, kitted out after being registered and still work out much cheaper than a new Camper import.

The Amescador, as the Ames Camper was known, was built during the 1970s. Three styles of roof were available: the old style Westy pop-top roof; the Martin Walter side-hinged elevating Dormobile roof; or a fixed high top which ran for two-thirds of the length of the Bus from the rear.

The most distinctive and different design feature on the Amescador Camper was the bed arrangement, which involved erecting a tent extension on the rear so that sleeping was part inside and part outside the vehicle! The spare wheel was moved to a front-mounted carrier to increase interior space, and a louvred side window was standard. There were three layout versions. EA could sleep four to five people and had a wardrobe and storage unit running from the sliding door to the rear, with another unit opposite where the spare wheel was normally mounted. By the sliding door behind the passenger was a sink, hob and fridge unit with a flap-down table on the opposite wall. Around this were a rear bench seat and a single seat behind the driver. The table could be used outside by attaching it to the fridge/hob unit and fitting an extending leg. HA was very similar but designed for two people. The four to five person AA version had the cooker/sink by the end of the rear bench, with a dinette style facing double seat and a table between. The upholstery for all models was finished in bright modern check fabrics, complementing the exterior colour, with matching curtains and covers for the cab seats.

By the late seventies Ames moved over to installing Westfalia kits on imported commercials, adding their own badge and logo to the vehicle. With the European Union expanding, and trade restrictions easing, Dutch people wanting Campers were now able to buy T25 Westfalias at competitive prices; although some LTs were converted into Campers by Ames, the easily available imported Westfalia Campers meant the demand was no longer there and production of the Amescador ceased.

The Amescador conversion featured here is owned by Cor Zeemans, from Holland. Built in April 1975 as a nine-seater Kombi, it was originally a bulkhead model, and exported to Holland to the Ames dealership. It is not known if it was used as a minibus, but the registration papers from 1976 show that by then it had been converted to a Camper, which involved removal of the bulkhead to create a walk-through interior, the fitting of a Westy pop top and an interior refit using the EA layout with the cooker and sink unit by the loading door. Microbus parts and trim such as the rubber strip on the bumpers were also added to upgrade the basic Kombi spec.

Very few Ames conversions survive, which makes this even more special. The logo on the cab door is the hand-painted version, as opposed to the vinyl stickers that were used later. Originally there was also a sticker on the front under the windscreen to match the one on the rear tailgate, but that has now gone due to rust repairs necessitating some repainting. The Bus is in very sound condition and has required little work other than attention to the front panel, a dent in the cab door, and repainting the bumpers. The dash had to be replaced with a padded version because the original dash had been hacked about to fit a radio. A Brink (Dutch brand) towing hitch has also been fitted.

For the tent extension a frame holds the tailgate in position and supports the base.

The frame support for the wooden base as viewed from underneath.

The tent is draped around the frame and held in place with guys, as can be seen in the close-up shots. Note the ventilation 'windows' on each tent side.

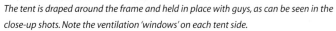

Amescador

The large sleeping space can be more easily seen without the tent in place. Note the shaped rear side cabinets to maximize sleeping width.

The rear side cabinets have open storage areas underneath – perfect for those bedtime accessories like a torch!

Matching fabric seat covers are part of the Amescador look.

An Amescador name badge is affixed to the rear tailgate above the handle.

An Amescador logo is painted on the front cab door; later models had a vinyl sticker.

The rear view shows the layout arrangement clearly, and the open storage shelf above the rear deck. The modern-looking bright upholstery, with matching curtains, is fully original and very different to the browns and beiges found on many UK Campers during the seventies.

The table can also be attached to the sink/cooker/cool box unit for use outside or with the optional side awning.

The rear seat, table and extra board lay flat …

… to form a second double bed.

arcomobil

arcomobil

The 62C model was a non-walk-through version with the cooker sited across the front bulkhead.

für alle Freunde der Ferne

Frau Mehl can be seen in the top picture; the detachable boat-shaped fixed-roof version can be seen in the lower picture. The caption translates colloquially as 'For all lovers of the great outdoors.'

Arcomobil Campers were established in Stuttgart, Germany, around 1960 by Arnold Mehl, initially using bulkhead models. It was very much a family business with wife Erika Mehl even appearing in their brochures! They produced high-quality cabinet-built conversions and Arcomobil Campers were also among the first to offer an elevating roof for a VW, the design of which is distinctive and unusual. Elevating roofs were fitted to sunroof Buses supplied by VW, minus the canvas and sliding gear; no roof cutting was therefore necessary and so the full VW warranty applied. When raised, the roof moves forwards and up, so there is an overhang at the front, and fold-up wooden sides secure it in place. Another version had an easily removable boat-shaped high top, which also fitted over the roof hole in factory sunroof models, but it is not known if any of these still exist.

Wood panelling and headliner, like that used by Westfalia, was standard and the spare wheel was front mounted to create more interior space. The company prided itself on tailoring or adapting their interiors to customer requirements, including the type of wood used or specially designed cabinets, but there were three basic interior layouts – the Arcona, Arcona C62 (with a traditional dinette layout) and the Arcomobil Pullman. All were available in fixed roof or elevating roof formats. A self-install kit version of the interior was also available, known as the Aria. As well as VW base units, Arcomobil also converted Ford, Mercedes, Tempo, Citroën and Renault vans.

Early versions had the cooker across the front bulkhead, with a single seat behind the driver and a washing unit by the load door. A wardrobe was sited just inside the rear load door, with the rear bench seat and table making a traditional dinette arrangement.

The Pullman, introduced in 1964, used the walk-through layout. Behind the driver was a hanging wardrobe; to the side of this was a large crockery and utensils cupboard, on top of which the cooker was mounted, facing towards the load doors. A single toiletry cabinet was sited by the front load door. A bench seat, with storage underneath, ran under the window to meet the rear bench seat, also with storage underneath. A swivel table, mounted on the under-window seat, allowed for a variety of table positions. An alternative layout had the under-window seat running full length to the rear bulkhead, with a single seat sited opposite, just inside the rear load door. With this arrangement the table was mounted at the rear between the single and bench seats. Extra storage was in the rear roof cupboard, on top of the wardrobe, and around the elevating roof. An open-slatted, useful storage unit was also mounted on the rear load door.

Another view of the unusual high roof option (and Frau Mehl); the rear window is just visible.

Matthias Meyer's 1965 Arcomobil Pullman.

The walk-through cab on the Pullman version
is a very useful feature.

By mounting the spare wheel on the front, extra
living space is created inside.

The roof has a small window in both the front
and rear sections.

An open storage unit is sited on the rear load
door. Note the birch panels used throughout.

Beneath the cooker is a crockery and utensils
cupboard; the crockery and utensils set here is
the original supplied equipment – even then, a
filter coffee maker was an essential item!

The swivel table is mounted on the side
seat base. There is also storage space beneath
the seating and above the windows.

Wood panelling is used throughout.

The Arcomobil pictured is owned by Matthias Meyer and is a 1965 Arcomobil Pullman, complete with the original crockery and utensils as supplied with the Bus. Matthias has substituted the single seat, originally with the Bus, for an Arcomobil full rear bench, but apart from that everything is original.

Very few Arcomobils survive (probably because comparatively few were built), but this mint 1967 version is now in the UK and currently owned by Steve Nolan. The layout differs slightly from the brochure layouts, in that the cooker is mounted on top of the unit by the load door and not on the large kitchen cupboard. The top flaps over the walk-through section to meet the matching Formica-topped kitchen unit, making a large L-shaped work surface area. On the side of the cooker unit, by the door, is a small pouch to hold two camping chairs. These slight differences are all original and it is likely that this is an example of a customer requesting some individual refinements.

The Bay Window Arcomobils kept broadly the same design for the cabinet work and layout, with the wardrobe behind the driver and the large kitchen cabinet to its side. The cooker was stored on top of this when travelling and was placed across the gangway on the kitchen cabinet and water cabinet sited by the sliding door. This cabinet housed a removable circular water container with gravity tap. A long bench seat ran under the window with a rear single seat just inside the sliding door. A long rectangular table was sited next to the single seat and extended into the back above the engine bay. The same elevating roof design continued, although a slightly longer version, without the distinctive rear overhang, was available.

When the son-in-law, Gerhard Grau, took over running the business around 1971, the conversion became known as the Grawomobil. Production ceased around 1979, but Arcomobil elevating roofs have been seen on early T25 Campers.

The roof pushes up and forwards …

… and wooden sides flap down to lock it in position.

Interior views of Steve Nolan's 1967 Arcomobil – the walk-through flap-top can be clearly seen.

The 1969 Arcomobil kept the same roof design.

This 1972 Grawomobil roof lifts straight up.

This 1976 model has the usual style of roof and the original two-tone paintwork option.

The **VOLKSWAGEN KOMBI VAN CARAVANETTE**
...a luxury holiday home on wheels

In 1958, at the same time that VW Australia was formed, Lanock Motors, a Sydney based VW dealership, began marketing a camping conversion known simply as the VW Kombi Van Caravanette.

The conversion was very well appointed, containing a spirit cooker, icebox fridge, wardrobe, water tank and dinette style seating that laid out to form the bed. Storage was ample. An optional tent awning was also available. Very few of these have survived, but the 1958 model pictured here, owned by Bill Moore, is in almost fully original condition and has been lovingly restored.

The only item still to source is the original brass sail track so that Bill can get an original striped annexe made up for it. The Bus was in fair shape when purchased, except for sills under the doors that were replaced, holes at the front for a non-original indicator set-up and flared rear guards to cover wide rims. It was originally the one colour, but Bill decided to two-tone it, using a local GM brown. The Bus is affectionately called the Paddle Pop, which is a local two-colour ice cream in Australia.

The original motor and gearbox were rebuilt and Bill has just added flashers at front and rear, due to 'too many clowns never looking for semaphores!' The original semaphores are still wired up and work, however.

The interior has original curtains, upholstery and cabinet work, all in excellent condition. Cupboard units were painted white with varnished wood doors.

The spirit cooker is housed in a metal-lined section of the cabinet for safe use.

The example pictured here dates from 1959 and is owned by Graham Darlington, who plans to restore it. Still in its original colour of Mango Green, most of the interior is intact, although in need of lots of work and TLC!

The Camper requires a full restoration both outside and inside, but will be well worth it as so few are known to have survived intact.

Sometime in the early sixties bullet style indicators were fitted as an upgrade, and mains hook-up and 240V interior lighting and power points were added. It has some differences from the 1958 version in that it has a sink unit where the cooker was and a door-mounted cabinet for the cooker; other than that it is essentially the same.

Two bench seats were arranged dinette style round a table, which lay down between the seats to form the bed. In this version, inside the front loading door at the end of the bench seat, was a sink unit with a manual pump tap and the cooker was mounted on the rear load door. Just inside the rear load door at the end of the rear seat was a large wardrobe with a light at the top above the door, with a mirror mounted on the side above the bench seat. The gas bottle was stored at the bottom of the wardrobe with a flexible pipe to supply gas to the cooker. A chrome rail was fitted above the mirror. In the rear were two storage cabinets, a large one and a smaller one at the very rear. Opposite these was a metal-lined cool box with a locking handle and ice tray complete with drain hole for placing a bag of ice (readily obtainable at most service stations) to keep food fresh and chilled. Upholstery had cloth one side and vinyl on the reverse and all units were painted in white, whilst the doors for the units were plain varnished wood.

Despite the rough condition of the Bus and its interior, Graham knows it is a rare model and, although the work required to bring it to the standard of Bill Moore's example is quite daunting, it will be well worth it as there are very few of these early camping conversions still around.

The headliner is wood ply, like early Westfalias. Note the light above the wardrobe door.

Dining mode.

Next to the load door is a sink unit with a water carrier for the manual tap stored underneath.

Reversible cushions, with vinyl side panels, lay out to form the bed using the table and bench seats. The upholstery shown is believed to be original.

The cooker unit is mounted on the rear load door and the gas bottle stored in the wardrobe, with a flexible pipe to connect the two.

The metal-lined cool box cabinet, with storage over. Note the clasp handle to ensure the door does not fly open!

The cool box has a separate section designed to hold an ice bag, with a drip tray and drain hole.

THE ADVENTURER: AUSTRALIA'S OWN CAMPMOBILE

Three versions of the Campmobile were available from VW Australia in the seventies: the Cruiser, the Adventurer and a Dormobile manufactured under licence.

If the US found problems importing enough Westfalia conversions to meet demand, Australia found it even more difficult. VW Australia was established at Clayton, Victoria, in 1958 and by 1961 had moved from assembling CKD (completely knocked down) kits into full-scale production with their own presses and local suppliers of components. They produced their own versions of the Campmobile, based on Westfalia designs, and, with the return to CKD assembly in 1968 they launched an Australian version of the Campmobile called the Adventurer. This was available in three versions: the Adventurer, the Adventurer Traveller and the Adventurer Deluxe. The conversions were carried out by E. Sopru and Company in conjunction with Volkswagen Australia.

All featured as standard kangaroo bars, front-mounted spare wheel, and a pop-top style elevating roof running over the living and rear areas. A hinged skylight (with VW logo) was fitted into the elevating roof. The interior was simple but effective, with units finished in wipe-clean light-coloured melamine. A rear bench seat converted to a double bed by using a rock-and-roll style mechanism. Along the driver's side opposite the sliding door were a tall cupboard for hanging space with a drawer under and mirror fixed to the side, a sink unit with pumped water supply (and hotplate for the Deluxe) and twin storage lockers at the rear. The table fixed to the section which housed the sink unit and a fluorescent light was sited above the sink. A roof cupboard was mounted at the rear. The 10gal (45.5ltr) water tank was mounted under the floor and filled from outside.

The Adventurer was the economy model with no cooker or fridge and standard equipment was as above, but included 240V mains hook-up and a fire extinguisher.

The Traveller also included a two-burner gas hob, and gas/electric fridge in a unit sited by the sliding door behind the front passenger seat, external side access door for the gas bottle and regulator, roof rack, retractable side step and portable box seat between the front cab seats.

The Deluxe featured a 240V hot plate next to the sink and bench seat, a 240V power point, an extra fluorescent light in the rear, a fold-down exterior table with bottle rack and cloth trim for the seats and side walls.

Other accessories included mosquito net sets, tent awning, a screened sliding window, grill covers, headlight guards, rear window demister, sun visor, and towbar. Also available, for those wanting real Outback or desert adventure, was an optional dust-free air cleaner, which was mounted on the roof at the rear of the vehicle.

VW Australia could also prepare European spec versions of their Campmobiles for overseas tourist delivery.

THE ADVENTURER DELUXE CAMPER

The vehicle featured here is a 1975 Adventure Deluxe, owned by Ade Pitkin. After a holiday in Australia he discovered rust-free Buses at a price he could afford and, on returning home, set about an Internet search. Finally he came across this Kombi Camper and after viewing digital images from every angle possible he took a leap of faith and bought it! The Bus had originally been owned by a local church near Brisbane and used for youth club activities. It was eventually sold on and had a partial engine rebuild before being sold on again. In the past three years of ownership the Bus has been trouble-free and the interior well suited to family use. Being the Deluxe Adventurer model, it features the electric ring at the end of the sink unit. The cooker unit is normally removed; not only is it in need of some refurbishment, it takes up too much valuable living space!

That apart, the interior is in excellent condition. The panels and units are all finished in pale blue and Ade says he especially likes the handy mirror on the wardrobe side, which hinges out above the sink and is ideal for shaving and so on.

An opening roof vent, complete with VW logo, is a neat touch.

The external elevating roof strut arrangement, folding out of the roof can be clearly seen.

The water tank is slung under the floor.

The full length wardrobe, with drawer under, has a handy vanity mirror that hinges out from the side, above the sink.

The cooker and cool box unit are sited inside the sliding door on the bulkhead, but are normally removed to create extra living space.

The gas bottle is accessed through an external side door. The adjacent plastic filler cap is for topping up the fresh water tank.

The Deluxe model features an electric hotplate ring next to the drainer.

Interior panels are also finished in pale blue to match the cabinet work. Note the extra storage above the linen cupboard and in the roof.

The wardrobe, sink/hob unit, linen storage and other cabinets are all finished in pale blue laminate. The pull-out bed gives ample sleeping space. Padded headrests on the cab seats are a standard feature for the Deluxe model.

THE CAMPMOBILE ADVENTURER

This 1975 Kombi Campmobile is the economy Adventurer model, imported to the UK by Recycling VWs, who specialize in sourcing Australian Buses and Campers. It features Roo bars with mountings for the spare wheel, sun visor, cab roof rack, side opening windows and an elevating roof.

E. Sopru also produced a version for VW Australia called the Cruiser. This featured a single seat, side wall-mounted foldaway table and rear bench seat. The rear seat and dining table were used to make up the bed. A large hanging cupboard was sited on the sliding door side at the rear with shelving at the end facing into the living area. There was also a roof cupboard. By the sliding door behind the passenger seat was a unit housing the sink, a two-burner cooker and the fridge. A pull-out shelf/worktop on the front gave extra space for washing or food preparation. An elevating roof was optional and the spare wheel was normally carried on a front-mounted roof rack.

Sopru also prepared Dormobiles, under licence, especially for the Australian market. Instead of the front seat cooker arrangement found on UK versions there was a fold-out two-burner hob and grill in a unit by the sliding door just behind the passenger seat. The spare wheel was mounted on the front, the elevating roof canvas was single colour, not striped, and cabinet work was in Nomad Walnut with tan trim, but, apart from that, the layout and specifications were the same as for UK Dormobiles. Options for all Sopru Campers included tow bars, mosquito net sets, a retractable side step, a screened sliding window by the dining table, a 12V oscillating fan, portable picnic sets including table and folding chairs, mains hook-up, twin battery system, cab roof rack, and air conditioning.

An unusual feature is the roof-mounted extra air filter, which suggests that the Bus was to be used in the extreme dust or sand conditions of the Australian Outback.

The Adventurer interior is more basic, with the large wardrobe, sink unit and pull-out bed. The table flaps up from the front of the sink unit for use. The cabinets are finished in pale grey laminate.

A 1976 Sunliner conversion.

A small flap-up worktop/table is mounted on the bulkhead by the sliding door.

Sunliner elevating roofs have a similar external strut arrangement to the Sopru Campers.

The Sunliner logo is painted onto the front of the roof section.

The single seat has a sink unit at its rear, with water and gas bottles stored in the base.

Marine ply cabinets are fitted with sliding doors.

The side cabinet by the sliding door extends all the way to the rear of the vehicle.

Vinyl-covered boards fold out to form a large, solid roof bed.

The later Trakka models featured a Devon style swing-out cooker.

Other 1970s Australian conversions included models by the following:

Lanock Motors

Lanock Motors were the first importers of VWs to Australia, in 1953. As well as the early camping conversions, they also contracted a company to convert Bay Window Buses and fit a fibreglass high roof.

Noosa Conversions

Based in Noosa, Queensland, Noosa Conversions produced Campers from around 1976. Interior fitting was similar to the Sopru Campmobiles but used fibreglass rather than wood for units. The units ran down the side opposite the sliding door and consisted of a three-burner Tutor gas hob, an Electrolux three-way fridge and storage units. A fibreglass water tank was slung under the vehicle and a removable cupboard unit was sited just inside the sliding door. The elevating roof was squarer shaped than the Campmobile versions.

SunCamper

SunCamper conversions started around 1977; the company is still in business today.

Sunliner

Sunliner Campers used a full length fibreglass roof with an integral roof rack over the cab area. Fittings were finished in marine ply, but were quite basic as can be seen in the Camper shown here. This Bus is rust-free and solid, and, because Sunliner Campers are rarely seen outside Australia, the new owners intend refurbishing the interior and woodwork to keep the Sunliner layout and feel.

Trakka

Trakka produced conversions from around 1973 featuring a water tank under the rear seat, a plastic sink and drainer, kitchen and storage units along one side, and four-post bull bars. The low profile full length elevating roof was reinforced with steel along the sides.

The advent of the T25 moved Camper conversions on the VW base model into a new era of luxury, with the result that the 1980s Campervans bore little resemblance to the spartan interiors of the fifties, the cabinet crafted wood interiors of the sixties, or the brown and orange interiors of the seventies. The eighties saw an upsurge of interest in a fully fitted self-contained, well-appointed Camper, and by the end of the eighties sales of motorhomes in the UK had nearly doubled, reaching 4,267 units.

Auto-Sleeper, based near Broadway in Worcestershire, were already a well-established motorhome converter by the time they brought VW-approved versions into their range in 1988, with the VX 50 (elevating roof), VHT (fixed high roof) and VT 20 (economy model).

Specifications were very high and a far cry from the basic Campers of the past – this was camping and travelling in style! The VX 50 and VHT models featured optional cab swivel seats and snack table to make an extra dinette area, and had cooking and washing facilities under the windows opposite the load doors. This included a three-way gas/electric fridge with a freezer compartment, stainless steel sink, two-burner cooker, storage unit and a chemical toilet. The VT 20 had a slightly different arrangement with cooker, sink and fridge behind the driver's seat and featured a U-shaped dinette arrangement with seating under the window at the end of these units as well as the rear bench seat. The VT 20 also featured the elevating roof.

For 1989 Auto-Sleeper offered just two versions – the Trident, with a permanent, aerodynamic high top roof, and the Trooper, with an elevating roof. These 1989 models featured the twin headlamp front grille and the new style bumpers and front spoiler. Both featured the same high level of specification, the only real difference being fixed or elevating roof options. These have gone on to become one of the most popular names in contemporary VW Campers, and the names Trooper and Trident have carried on through the T4 and T5 platforms.

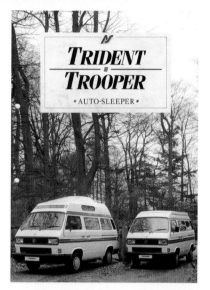

THE 1989 TRIDENT

The Trident model featured here is quite unusual in that it is built on a Syncro base, featuring front and rear diff locks. Only 2,108 RHD Syncros were actually produced and very few were officially kitted out as Campers. This version is finished in Pastel White (L90D) and it features the distinctive Auto-Sleeper decals and striping. The interior is well laid out with a three-way fridge (with freezer compartment), stainless steel sink, two-burner grill/cooker that folds away to create table or worktop space, a chemical toilet in its own storage space and ample cupboard and

wardrobe storage areas. A sliding window is fitted with a flyscreen. The interior is fully carpeted, the upholstery is plush and comfortable and the Trident version also features a roof bed in the fixed high top space. A roof rack is accessed by a ladder mounted on the rear tailgate; this model also has a fold-down spare wheel carrier fitted to the rear and bull bars on the front. It's interesting to note that the top of the range fitted 'extras' at the time included wheel trims, facia storage tray, intermittent wipe, padded steering wheel, heated rear window and vanity mirror with integral light, whilst warm air heating was still optional, as was a swivel front seat.

T4 CAMPERS

With the advent of the T4 generation in 1990 Auto-Sleeper began to extend further their range of VW based Campers, and their models began to rival famous US motorhomes in terms of equipment and specification. The Trident and the Trooper remained the volume sales vehicles, with the Trident continuing to be the fixed high top model and the Trooper the elevating roof version. The Topaz was an LWB version with a kitchen and bathroom complete with shower at the rear of the vehicle, whilst Clubman, Gatcombe, Sherbourne and Medallion were all coach-builds that offered luxury specifications, including showers, ovens, microwaves and satellite televisions – a world away from the original conception of the Camping Box interiors!

THE 1999 TROOPER

The Trooper was the elevating roof version, and like the T4 Trident, took motorhomes to new standards in comfort and luxury. Standard fittings included electric hook-up, swivel front seat, three-way fridge with freezer compartment, blown-air heater, stainless steel sink with electric tap, waste and fresh water tanks, dual-access wardrobe, Porta Potti, pull-out double bed, two tables that could be mounted in a variety of positions, smoke alarm, CD player, cutlery and china for four, two-burner hob/grill and plush upholstery. The Bus pictured here was bought new in 1999 by Russ Dowson and he liked it so much that three years later he traded it in for a 2002 model! A long time Split Screen enthusiast, Russ commented:

It's a modern version of a Practical Classic – and when my Split Pick-Up truck is finally restored we will take both to shows! The Pick-Up is my hobby, my T4 is a lifestyle. It's great to come home from work, chuck in the mountain bikes and head off, even in winter. It opens up a whole new world beyond the summer and it's so nice to be warm when driving or sleeping! I just love the luxury and comfort.

The Clubman features a rear-sited kitchen and built-in TV.

A luxurious kitchen and fitments, plus a bathroom with built-in shower at the rear, are the hallmarks of the Topaz model.

The interior of the coach-built Sherbourne looks more like a plush hotel room than a Camper interior!

The swivel passenger seat makes a cosy sitting room.

The fridge has a built-in freezer compartment.

The optional pull-out awning is a very useful accessory.

Two tables provide flexible dining arrangements.

The kitchen units and wardrobe are all sited along one side.

T5 CAMPERS

Trident and Trooper continue through into the new T5 platform, introduced in 2003. A glance at the interior design and layout reveals sophistication and class – a new generation of VW Campers for a new generation of Campers who demand more than a field with a tap! *Which Motorcaravan* praised the conversions, stating, 'Many will love its new-found style and rejoice in the convenience of the nationwide Auto-Sleepers dealer network and assured resale values. This new Trooper bears no resemblance to its dated predecessor in its furniture style or galley fittings.'

Auto-Sleeper are based near Broadway in Worcestershire.
Telephone: 01386 853338; website: www.auto-sleepers.co.uk.
They also support an active owners' club.

Bilbo Campers started life in the back streets of Amsterdam in the mid-seventies. Using second-hand Dutch Police and Army Buses, which were readily available, David Latham and his wife Moira found there was a market building Campers. Initially, all the work was done by just the two of them, with David on the jigsaw and Moira on the sewing machine!

After doing this for a couple of years, honing their skills and designs, they returned to England in 1977 and rented a garage in Reigate, Surrey, from which to continue the business; soon after they moved to a small part of their present site in South God-stone. Their Bay Window conversion was known as the Marlfield, after the road on which the business was sited.

This is one of the very few Bilbo conversions on a Bay Window Bus

known to survive. Built in 1978 as a Kombi, it was used by the Dutch military before being imported and converted by Bilbo in 1985. The Marlfield conversion featured very modern materials and it is quite strange seeing a modern style interior in a seventies Bus. It is fitted with dual Captain's front seats, both with rotating bases, although the passenger seat is probably the only really useful one. It has a walk-through interior, leading to an electric pump tap and sink and two-burner gas hob. Under the sink is a portable 2.2gal (10ltr) water container into which the pump is fitted. There is a gas bottle in the cupboard to the left of the hob. Under the hob is a two-way fridge. The 'white' carpet, however, is not a very practical colour! The bed is a fold-down type, and

there is another double bed in the pop-top roof. Under the lower bed is additional storage, as well as some to the side. The wardrobe sits to the rear and also houses the electric hook-up fuse box. Sockets are situated throughout the van. There is a variety of lights around the van, including a fluorescent one that runs off the electric hook-up as well as battery-powered ones. There is also a roof vent for additional ventilation, as well as louvred side windows. Alex Muir, the current owner, is very proud of his Camper, and says, 'It's style on wheels. I love driving him around, and I always come away smiling after even the shortest journeys. He's comfortable inside at night too, with lots of storage and a well put-together interior. I'm 6ft 5in tall and there is plenty of room even for me!'

The layout can clearly be seen here: note the roof bed boards, upper rear locker, rear wardrobe unit, mains electric sockets and an assortment of lighting!

Though both front seats swivel, the layout means that only the passenger seat is practical for everyday use.

The kitchenette is arranged down one side and consists of a two-burner hob and grill, sink unit and electric fridge. Melamine gives a clean, light and modern feel to the cabinet work.

The Westpoint Plus elevating roof was Bilbo's own design and construction.

The Bilbo conversions name badge is affixed to the tailgate.

The roomy upper berth with electric light.

The lower berth is pull-out style.

Bilbo's T25 conversion, known as the Marlfield after the road where the works were sited, marked their entry into the mainstream camping conversion business.

During the 1980s Bilbo continued mainly converting second-hand vans, but in 1987 they began to convert new vehicles. In the early 1990s they gained VW approval and today continue to turn out well-appointed, popular conversions.

Their T25 range comprised the Arragon, Arragon Coda and Arragon 2, Marlfield and Weekender. Customers would specify upholstery, coachwork, curtains and flooring to create their own look inside.

Keeping the name of the Bay Window forerunner, the Marlfield was the first of their new T25 conversions. Brazilian Virola-faced 12mm ply was used for its cabinet work. The Arragon line was the top end of the range, using basically the same layout as the Marlfield, but with more accessories and fitments such as twin reading spotlights, a sliding single seat and front swivel seats as standard and with the option of a more comprehensive kitchen area. Arragon cabinet work was initially finished in beech or light grey laminate, but Arragon 2, based on new T25 models, used a new style furniture laminate material imported from Europe that was extremely hard-wearing. It was finished in light grey with dark grey plastic trim for all edges. Other refinements included storage over the engine, a slide-out cutlery tray and a non-slip seat housing a Porta Potti. Safety was high on the agenda with fire-retardant materials and foam, and rear seat belts as standard.

The Arragon model was the top end of the range in the 1980s.

The Arragon 2 marked the move to a new style of coloured laminate cabinet work.

The aptly named Weekender has a well-appointed multi-use interior.

The Weekender was a multipurpose conversion, which was both spacious and luxurious. A full width rear seat pulled out to form a large double bed. A unit behind the front passenger housed a cooker, wash bowl, water pump and utensil storage. Behind the driver was another single seat, which stored an optional 12V cool box, with a flap top to make a double seat across the gangway.

Bilbo's also developed their own range of roofs that could be fitted to their conversions. The Astron was a fixed high top that housed another double bed, with optional front and rear lockers, and could be fitted to any Bilbo T25 conversion. The Westpoint was a side-hinged three-quarter length elevating roof with a front-moulded over-cab section to give extra storage. The Westpoint plus was a full length version of the same roof. Both could be fitted with the optional 'upstairs' package consisting of twin-section double bed, trim, curtains and reading lamp. The Westpoint Plus could also be fitted with an extra child's berth over the front cab. The Westpoint elevating roofs could be fitted to both the T25 and Bay Window models, and could also be fitted to

customer's existing vehicles. The roof was strong enough to have surfboard bars fitted.

T4 CAMPERS

The T4 range consisted of four models. The Kompak featured a passenger swivel seat with the unit housing the cooker, sink and portable fridge running along the sidewall behind the driver and a wardrobe in the rear. The Breakaway used the same furniture but with front swivel for both cab seats, a plumbed-in sink, 50ltr fridge, fresh water and waste tanks, two multi-position tables and mains hookup. The Celeste was the top of the range Camper with a 65ltr fridge and two-burner hob with warming oven and grill, as well as extra storage cupboards. The Nektar was slightly different in that it was built on a long wheelbase T4, though an SWB version was also available. The kitchen was sited in the rear of the vehicle, with a wardrobe opposite; the versatile interior layout meant that one person could be resting on a single bed whilst another used the table or prepared a meal. All models had elevating roofs or the Skyliner high top could be fitted

at no extra cost. The comprehensive options reflected the changes in motor caravan and Campervan use generally; the days of roughing it were long past. Options included power-assisted elevating roof mechanisms, bike racks, solar panels, exterior shower unit and there were also options for wheelchair ramps and clamps.

T5 CAMPERS

The same excellent build quality and high specifications are found in Bilbo's new range based on the T5, comprising the Komba, Nexa and Celex. *Which Motorcaravan*, in November 2004, tested the five VW based Campers then available in the UK: Auto-Sleeper Trooper, Bilbo's Celex, Devon's Moonraker 5, Reimo Legacy and the VW California. The Celex, based on the T4 Celeste, was voted the winner, with the declaration, 'With the best bed, the best kitchen, the best dining arrangements and the best roof, the Celex is a worthy winner.' From back-street converter to award-winning business, the new Bilbo Campers have set the standard for a whole new generation of VW conversions.

Three types of roof were available as options: Astron High Top; Westpoint; Westpoint plus.

The new T5 Nexa is based on the T4 Nektar, with kitchen at the rear.

Bilbo's Design are based in Godstone, Surrey.
Telephone: 01342 892499; website www.bilbos.com

Getaway car.

Get it any way you want it.

A Campmobile kit could transform a Panel Van into a holiday home on wheels, as can be seen in pictures from this 1964 brochure.

To make the De Luxe Kit Super De Luxe

A range of tents and tent extensions were available, including shower sections and a tent fitted to a roof deck!

Campers, motorhomes and recreational vehicles (RVs) have always been serious business in the USA and Canada, especially with so much wilderness to explore. Westfalia Campers had been available in North America as specific Export models since 1956 (see Chapter 38), and, by 1961, with the introduction of SO 34, demand far exceeded supply. This shortage was met head on by VWoA (Volkswagen of America) and VW Canada, who manufactured kits that could be bought, ready installed, by a VW dealership on a new or used vehicle or installed DIY at home. The US version was marketed as the Campmobile – a name that later became synonymous with Westfalia Export models for North America, whilst the VW Canada version was entitled the Canadiana. Although the kits show distinct Westfalia influence in design, materials and layout, they do have their own characteristics and in no way deserve the nickname 'Westfakia'! Being built in the home of

the RV, the US Campmobiles were actually better equipped and, some would say, offered more comfort and luxury, whilst the Canadiana was more basic but with some classy touches of woodwork. Ideally designed for Kombis or Microbuses, kit versions for Panel Vans were also available and included small side windows, based on standard RV parts and similar to those used on EZ Campers.

THE CAMPMOBILE

In 1963 *Hot Rod* magazine road-tested and reviewed the latest range of VW models, including the newly available Campmobiles:

With the almost sensational boom in motorized Campers, installed on anything that is self-powered, it stands to reason VW would have such equipment. In fact, they were among the first. A handful of attractive Campers, fitted out in Germany, made their appearance some years ago in VW dealerships but they had price tags of over

$3,000. Thriftier owners converted their own but now a series of six Campmobile kits are available to be fitted to existing panels, Kombis and Microbuses.

A basic and deluxe version was available for each model, with some very interesting accessories …

The basic kit consisted of five small gear-operated screened windows (for the Panel Van version), birch panels for walls and roof, seating with storage under, vinyl floor covering, folding table with extension leaf, loading door shelf units, wardrobe with mirror, two wall-mounted lights (very similar to the clamshell variety used on the SO 23), magazine cabinet, rear linen cupboard, small rear corner unit, and a shelf behind the rear bench and on the front bulkhead. Cushioning was available in either red or turquoise and finished in nylon or vinyl; soil-resistant co-ordinated check curtaining, with ties, was included.

The Deluxe version added a water pump and cool box unit, with flap for a washing bowl, by the loading door, a two-burner gas stove (which stood on a flap-up shelf on the rear loading door), and a chemical toilet, stored under the single seat.

Hot Rod describes the optional accessories as extras that 'will permit the prospective outdoorsman to rough it in even greater comfort'. A huge pull-out sun awning with roll-down sides could be mounted above the loading doors and you could also specify an 8ft square (2.4m square) free-standing Cabana tent. The roof rack with ladder doubled as a sun deck and the Campette option consisted of a tent fitted onto this for penthouse style sleeping. There was even an option for a 25gal (114ltr) shower unit and shower enclosure!

VWoA proudly invited customers to, 'Take your next vacation in a Campmobile. It's a very moving experience. No hotel, motel, resort or restaurant bills. No reservations, packing or tipping porters. Great for people who'd rather look at scenery than at No Vacancy signs. Great, too, for quietly stealing away (people can't visit you if they can't find you).'

Send this kit to camp

Campmobile kits were offered as conversions by dealerships on new or used vehicles, or for DIY assembly.

VWoA continued to market its own Campmobile until 1972, when Westfalia models specifically geared to the US market began to be produced (*see* Chapter 38). The name Campmobile, originally used by Westfalia, was also adopted by VW Australia and South Africa to market their own versions of VW Campers.

THE CANADIANA

VW Canada also retailed its own Camper, very similar to the US version, from 1963, called the VW Canadiana Vacationer. It was more basic than the US version, with birch wood panelling for walls and roof, a two-thirds bench seat behind the front bulkhead with a shelf behind it, a table and rear bench seat, also with a shelf behind. There was a wardrobe with mirror at the end of the rear bench by the door, and a linen closet behind this in the rear, with a smaller cupboard in the corner by the tailgate. A mattress lay over the rear deck on top of a wooden frame with storage under. The high position double bed used the table and seat to meet the mattress in the rear load area. The bulkhead seat had curved lines and the edges were finished with chrome stripping to match the table edge. Bakelite handles and chrome hinges were used for cupboards. Another distinctive feature was the scalloped wood trim pelmet running round at curtain track height. Two

coat-hanging pegs were affixed above the windows opposite the loading doors and the central interior light was replaced with a circular fitting with a copper base. Curtains were Westy style check, although 'modern' fabrics with palm trees and bright designs were also used. Cushions were covered with abstract print, with one side covered with brown or black vinyl. A useful feature, supplied as standard, was a pull-out slide step under the load doors.

Another special feature of the Canadiana was the inclusion, as standard, of a Hupp gas heater, fitted in the base of the bulkhead seat, no doubt to cope with Canadian winters. The VW Camper's ability to cope with all conditions and all terrains was at the centre of VW Canada's PR material, which, apart from claiming some owners returned 35mpg, stated:

> The VW makes an ideal rolling cottage. Its rear-mounted engine gives you traction in mud or sand or down those backwoods roads. Being air cooled your VW engine will never need anti-freeze or water nor will it boil over. Torsion bar suspension can get you over the roughest terrain and no wonder the VW is popular with Safari people in Africa.

The Canadiana fitted the bill perfectly as a no-frills, affordable Camper for those who wanted to really tackle the Canadian wilderness!

Like the US Campmobile, the Canadiana could be bought as a kit for DIY assembly, or installed on customers' existing vehicles by a dealership. There was also an option for Panel Van conversion, though the VW Canada versions were normally Kombis.

Under the title 'Turn Your VW Window Van into a Rolling Cottage', this 1966 Canadiana brochure extolled the virtues of wilderness camping. Note the Hupp heater sited under the front bench seat – a standard item for the Canadiana!

THE 1963 CANADIANA CAMPER

The example featured here was built in January 1963, shipped via Vancouver and converted by VW Canada in Toronto. It was acquired in 2003 by Rob Kneisler, and, despite some modifications to the body, it is the only known Canadiana to survive intact. Sometime during the eighties an accident necessitated the fitting of a 1967 front including the dash, cab doors and front bumper. It has also had a 12V conversion and a 1600 engine fitted. That apart, the Bus is mainly original and rust-free. Sometime in 2002 the previous owner completely dismantled the original interior and, using the pieces as templates, faithfully reproduced the interior. The only difference is that birch veneer was used instead of the original oak. All the original bakelite handles, chrome stripping and hinges were refitted. The curtains are also original. Whilst the interior may not be an original Canadiana, it is as authentic as you can get and is an important part of the VW Camper story.

A retractable side step was standard equipment.

A storage area is provided in the rear deck under the mattress. Chrome hinges and bakelite handles are all original features

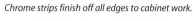

Chrome strips finish off all edges to cabinet work.

Dash-mounted fan is a cool period accessory!

The whole interior is panelled and finished in natural wood.

Note the scalloped pelmets, often known as gingerbread trim, a distinctive Canadiana feature.

Sleeping mode.

THE PITT MOTO-CARAVAN

One of the unsung pioneers of the motor caravan, who was a prime mover in developing the newly expanding UK motorhome market in the 1950s, was Peter Pitt. Not only was he responsible for one of the first full camping conversions on the VW base, and the first UK VW Camper, he was also instrumental in getting laws changed to put the motorhome on the same footing as a touring caravan.

Motor vehicles bought in the UK at this time were subject to purchase tax, but a motorhome was exempt from this. The regulations decreed that a motorhome had to be equipped with permanent fittings consisting of a dining area, beds, cooking equipment, wardrobe space and water-carrying facilities. (These regulations actually caused Danbury to redesign their initial conversion in 1964 to make the cooker 'permanent'.) Pitt designed his VW conversion in 1956, using a modular arrangement that was to become the Open Plan design used in the 1960s. However, UK regulations in the 1950s designated the VW Transporter as a commercial vehicle, which meant it was subject to a top speed restriction of 30mph as well as purchase tax!

In order to draw attention to this anomaly, Pitt took his VW Camper to the Royal Park at Windsor, knowing full well that 'commercial' vehicles were prohibited. The case came to court and the judgment ruled that Pitt's motorhome was not a commercial vehicle but should be classed as a private car. This resulted in two important things: firstly, a motorhome could now travel at the same speeds as private cars; and, secondly, purchase tax no longer applied (although Customs and Excise still had to inspect and approve conversions.).

This 1958 Camper is one of the earliest Pitt conversions and has recently been fully restored to the original condition. It has many of the distinctive features found on the later standard production models, with some interesting variations.

The fold-out, door-mounted cooker was an original Pitt design feature.

The maker's logo was fixed to the side cooker.

The rear bench seat is in two sections – the base of the section nearest the load door flaps down to make access easier when the table is in use.

The side cabinet has a flap-up shelf extension for a washing bowl or work surface.

The oak interior has been faithfully restored
and the basic layout remains unchanged.

Extra storage cupboards are built into the
bench seat backs.

The wardrobe has a curtained front with a gas
light mounted on its side.

A small vanity/toiletry cupboard, with fitted
mirror (here affixed to the door back), was
another distinctive Pitt design feature.

This 1963 model has been accessorized with a side step, jail bars, door handle protectors, and a
Westfalia style roof rack and ladder; the interior, however, is fully original.

The underfloor water tank was filled via a
hatch in the floor; this was later changed to a
water tank sited under the front bench seat to
reduce the risk of contamination when filling.

The original upholstery and curtaining are still
in good condition.

Despite using a VW for his first conversion, import duties made the vehicle more expensive than UK-produced vehicles, so Pitt initially concentrated on conversions based on Thames, Commer and Austin bases, although some VW conversions were built for customers. Pitt's conversions were at the forefront in design, and in 1959 he introduced to the market a GRP High Top and elevating roofs.

In 1960 Pitt reintroduced the VW into the range, using his open design interior. This comprised interlocking units that enabled a variety of layouts: it could be arranged as a dinette (seating eight), and made up into single, double or twin beds. A fold-down cooker was mounted on the rear loading door but there was no sink.

Pitt's major innovation this year, which took competitors by surprise, was a new style of elevating roof called the Rising Sunshine Roof. This spring-loaded design could be fixed in three positions, consisting of fully open at one end, half open or fully closed all round. Bunks could be installed to increase sleeping space. However, the only demonstrator models on show at the 1960 Motor Show with this feature were Commer and Thames conversions. Although the option was available for all the Pitt conversions, if any VW had such an option fitted none has survived.

In 1961 the Pitt Moto-Caravan Company merged with Canterbury Sidecars. Conversions were from then on carried out at the Canterbury Sidecars premises in Romford and marketed as Canterbury Pitt Conversions. The new VW version introduced that year featured an optional sink unit at the end of the rear bench seat, with a chassis-mounted 10gal (45.5ltr) water tank and push–pull pump delivery to the tap.

1963: THE VW CANTERBURY PITT OPEN PLAN MOTO-CARAVAN

Production moved to new premises at South Ockenden, Essex, and Pitt updated and refined the designs and layouts for the models introduced for 1963. The conversion was so successful that it remained basically unchanged over succeeding years until production ceased.

The sink unit was optional for all models and sited at the end of the rear bench. The pump handle, visible here, was sited on the bench facia.

The unit folds up and forwards to lock into position and the seat base/lid hinges back to form a drainer.

The cooker is the less common stainless steel version.

A mirror is mounted on the rear of the side-hinged toiletry cabinet.

The gas bottle was stored in the engine compartment and gas fed to the cooker via metal and flexible pipes.

A single curtained area at the rear, with fitted wooden hangers, forms the wardrobe.

The front bench seat was in two sections (double and single), allowing three different seating arrangements, with the front bench seat movable to under the windows to create more floor space. Double, single or twin bed layouts were all possible and children were accommodated with an optional stretcher cab bunk. There was also an optional adult forelong bunk, which ran along the side above the front seats/bed and into the cab.

A foldaway two-ring cooker/grill was mounted on the front loading door and housed in a cabinet that had a flap-down shelf door for the crockery and cutlery section beneath the cooker. The Kombi version had only a two-burner cooker as standard and fitted crockery and cutlery was optional for both Microbus and Kombi versions. The foldaway drainer/sink was optional on all models and was sited at the loading door end of the rear bench. The water tank was sited under the chassis and filled via a simple bath plug, which was positioned in the load floor just where people got in and out. (This arrangement increased the risk of contamination and in 1967 the tank was moved to under the front bench seat.) The gas cylinder was sited in the engine bay and gas was piped under the floor to the cooker. The author can still vividly remember the fear of carrying gas here when a gas cylinder had been overfilled in Afghanistan – and eventually opted to release half the contents manually before reinstalling the cylinder!

The Microbus version also featured as standard a compartmentalized storage area above the engine, accessed from the rear via two drawers, or from inside by a lift-up top; the sections at either end were accessed from the top. There was also a roof cupboard flanked by two side cupboards with small forward-facing doors for access. One of these was fitted with a vanity/shaving mirror on the inside. This equipment could be ordered for the Kombi as an extra. Cabinet work was normally finished in dark oak; Microbus versions were painted in two tone, whilst Kombi conversions were single colour.

THE CANTERBURY **VOLKSWAGEN** PITT·OPEN·PLAN MOTO-CARAVAN.. NOW WITH **DIVIDED GANGWAY** OPTIONAL EXTRA

✳ FOR EASY ACCESS ✳ GREATER CONVENIENCE

This new addition to the Canterbury Pitt range has been produced by popular demand. Step straight from the driving seat into the cabin . . . . . . enjoy complete access to the interior at all times. You can forget the weather with a divided gangway . . . . . . simply pull up - pop through, and the tea's on the table before you know it.

Divided gangway showing normal seating arrangement.

ONLY £25 EXTRA

Canterbury Industrial Products (Aveley) Ltd.
Arisdale Avenue, South Ockendon, Essex.
Tel - South Ockendon 3456
Cables - Cantacar

Divided gangway showing twin beds in position.   Divided gangway showing table in position.

The optional divided gangway version became available in 1965.

The 1965 brochure.

Brochures of the time focused on both versatility and freedom of 'Private Motoring in Hotel Comfort', urging potential buyers to

Go anywhere ... see everything, free from timetable restrictions and accommodation problems. No hotel bills for your family and friends ... there's plenty of room for all ... with your gear neatly stowed away in the ample locker and wardrobe space. Be free as a bird to wander as the mood takes you, stopping at will. Or, when not on pleasure bent, turn your caravan into a highly mobile office. The furniture swings into several self-locking arrangements with remarkable ease, or folds away to increase the low central floor space to 16sq ft so that your caravan becomes a willing work horse for the transport of bulky packages.

A slimline pop-top elevating roof was now available, which increased the overall height of the vehicle by only 3in (76mm). Another unique feature was the sun canopy, which fitted across the top of the open loading doors and was secured by straps across the roof to the opposite side of the body.

In 1965 a walk-through option was offered, designated as the Pitt Open Plan Divided Gangway. In 1967 the rather heavy elevating roof was redesigned to make it lighter and easier to erect.

This 1966 model was the standard version, without a sink. The seats have been re-covered.

A washing bowl sits in a special cut-out under the rear bench. Water is pumped by a Whale tap.

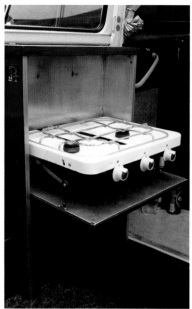

The cooker/grill is vitreous enamel – note the Pitt badge on the side.

The vanity mirror on later models was mounted on a pivoting wooden base on the door back.

Under the front bench seat is a handy bottle storage rack.

Both rear side sections have curtain screens with hanging racks. Rear storage is accessed from inside by using simple finger cut-outs.

At the rear is a roof storage cupboard. Vanity cupboards with flap-down doors are located in the sides of the curtained wardrobes.

THE END OF AN ERA

Sadly, Peter Pitt died in February 1969. The business arrangement was such that his designs were manufactured under licence, with the result that production of the Canterbury Pitt Moto-Caravan ceased around September that year. There had been a Bay Window conversion made (Peter Pitt had one for his own use), but numbers were small. The surviving example shown here has a new style of fold-down cooker attached to the bulkhead, which could also swing-out to be used standing up by the door. That apart, the layout remained very similar to before, including the distinctive side and roof cabinets by the rear seat. The interior cabinet work on this example has been painted blue at some point, but would have originally all been finished in oak. Although the interior is in a sad condition, it will be restored eventually and thus preserve another part of the VW Camper story.

The new style of Pitt cooker is mounted flat on the front bulkhead, and folded down for use.

The cooker can now swing-out, Devon style, for inside or outside use.

The rear bench is in three sections. Note the traditional style Pitt rear layout is still retained.

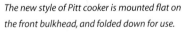

The vanity cabinet mirror on the cabinet door back is now hinged.

The washing bowl is still sited in a cut out under the rear bench

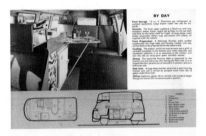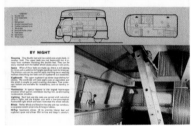

Not the prettiest of conversions but certainly spacious! The underfloor water tank is visible in this 1963 Brochure.

The unusual shaped table and kitchenette layout can be seen here.

Roller blinds were fitted to all windows; another distinctive HiTop feature.

Of all the conversions offered on a VW base, the HiTop model from Caraversions is perhaps one of the oddest looking! Based in London, Caraversions offered their new conversion, on a VW Kombi walk-through base, from 1962. Elevating roofs were beginning to be commonly available by this time, but the HiTop was the first conversion to fit a permanent high top to the VW base. As well as the distinctive and unusual shape of the roof with three banks of louvred windows on each side, the interior layout was also very different and well appointed. However, despite being very functional and giving permanent standing space, the external appearance was not especially aesthetic and one wonders what it must have been like to drive in a crosswind!

The high roof housed two adult-sized single beds (not bunks), with a fitted kitchen cupboard in the front section and a fitted clothes cupboard at the rear. A ladder allowed access to the bunks, whilst the cupboards were easily accessible by standing. Extra storage cupboards ran above the side windows, under the bunks. The kitchen unit was sited behind the driver and housed a large, circular, deep stainless steel sink served by pumped water from a 12gal (54.6ltr) tank slung under the floor and a 1.6cu ft gas Electrolux fridge fitted as standard. A curtained section next to the fridge housed the gas bottle. The cooker featured two burners and a grill, and was carried in the lower section of the roof's kitchen cupboard. For use, it was attached to the kitchen unit and hung over the driver's seat back in the cab. The upper section of the roof cupboard housed two saucepans, a kettle, frying pan, teapot and grill pan on the top shelf, with four place settings of large plates, small plates, bowls, cups, saucers and cutlery, all of which were supplied as standard.

At the end of the kitchen unit was a shaped Formica table, attached to the kitchen unit and with a single prop allowing maximum free floor space. Bed boards were stored above the engine and laid out over the rear seat and into the space above the engine to make a 6ft 3in by 4ft 6in (1.9m by 1.4m) double bed. A large hanging wardrobe was also sited in the rear. A flap-down Formica worktop/table was hinged behind the front passenger seat and a folding seat increased the seating area to allow seating for six. The full width rear bench seat had a drawer section in the centre with closed lockers either side of this. Windows were fitted with striped roller blinds and a one-piece curtain was provided for the front screen. Vynide was used for upholstery and side panels, while furniture was finished in Zebrano with mahogany doors and interiors, and polished aluminium framing and edge trim.

In 1964 a standard roof version of the Caraversion was introduced, identical in layout and fitment to the HiTop, but without all the units fitted into that roof and designed to accommodate two adults and one child. Very few HiTops were produced and only one surviving model has ever been recorded; perhaps buyers preferred the look of other conversions despite the high level of fixtures and fittings found as standard on the HiTop.

These shots, taken in Cornwall or Devon in the early sixties outside a Surf Shop, show a well-travelled Bus presumably owned by Australian Surfers.

Danbury Conversions were based in Chelmsford, Essex. They came later to the VW Camper scene, launching their Danbury Multicar in 1964, based on 1963 VW models; however, from the start it was quite distinctive in design. In October 1964 *Autocar* reported:

> So many different companies have tried dozens of layouts in their motor caravan designs that it would appear difficult for a newcomer to the industry to find a fresh approach. Danbury Conversions have succeeded, however, by concentrating on appearance and convenience in their Multicar caravan. They put its use as a road vehicle first and foremost, and the fittings do not detract from this in any way. Yet it is also a comfortable motor caravan when in camp.

THE MULTICAR

Conversions based on the Panel Van, Kombi and Microbus bulkhead models were all available to order; with the van version coming in at just £918 it represented real value for money in what was becoming a highly competitive market. It was also possible to specify loading doors on both sides for the Panel Van version, for access on both sides. Because windows had to be let into the Panel Van body, the Kombi, with its bigger factory-fitted windows, was a more popular model. Customers could also take their own vehicle to Danbury for conversion, which cost around £210 depending on requirements and vehicle condition.

Seating was somewhat different to the usual two benches facing a table dinette, in that a bench seat ran down the offside wall for daytime use. The table had two legs, stowed separately and was stored under the roof locker above the engine compartment when not in use. The table could also be used outside. The seat bases and cushions were laid out flat to make a roomy 6ft by 4ft (1.8m by 1.2m) double bed using the table top and boards. Children could be accommodated in the space above the engine compartment or on a front cab bunk and there was also the option of extra

adult bunks in the main area – though with no elevating roof space it must have been very cramped! The seat cushions were reversible with one side being cloth covered, and the other being wipe-clean leatherette. The vinyl headlining had foam insulation and the interior panels were lined with Vynide over a soft foam backing. Grey PVC was used for most of the interior coverings, and the curtains were on one continuous Silent Gliss rail. They tucked away at the rear when not wanted, leaving the windows clear. This meant that the van looked less of a 'holiday' vehicle when being used as a people carrier or load hauler.

Like Pitt's Open Plan design, all the fittings were detachable so that a variety of layouts was possible. The sink unit was sited at the end of the rear bench seat, but, as it was movable, the rear bench could be arranged as a full width seat. The cooker unit, containing a two-burner and grill cooker and storage cupboard, was just behind the front passenger seat. Both these were made as matching units resembling three-sided rectangular boxes, with the fourth side partly cut away. Initially both had detachable, instead of hinged, lids, which some found annoying, whilst others found they made excellent eating trays for the children! These free-standing units made it possible to cook indoors or from outside the van and there were even alternative waste pipes so that the sink could be positioned behind the driver. Water was carried in three 2gal (9ltr) polythene containers, and a feed pipe attached to the push–pull tap on the sink unit was put into whichever container was being used. Interestingly, UK Customs regulations of the time specified that equipment in a motor caravan must be fixed, so Danbury had to redesign the cooker to ensure it was secure, arranging for it to tip so as to give access to the Calor Gas bottle stored underneath.

Two other rectangular boxes, similar in size to the sink and cooker units, contained drawers and cubby holes respectively for the very comprehensive sets of cutlery and crockery supplied as standard. This

included a teapot, frying pan and saucepan – items not considered by other converters as standard! There was also a cool box and milk bottle rack.

The rail behind the rear seat could be removed to increase the capacity to carry long loads. A detachable hat rack, four coat hooks and three coat hangers with double hooks to secure them were fixed to twin rails at the rear of the vehicle to form a 'wardrobe'. Initially, Danbury again fell foul of Customs regulations, which decreed a cover should be fitted to enclose the coat hangers and bars, so Danbury simply designed and provided a transparent plastic curtain so that rear vision would not be obscured! Later this became a sliding fabric curtain. There was also a very useful storage pocket mounted inside the right-hand loading door.

Optional extras included two-tone finish, Philips radio, an electric clock, 6ft adult bunks, a larger cooker, and an external canopy that stretched above the open double loading doors and flapped back over the roof for securing.

By 1966 the Danbury Multicar had only had a few minor modifications and improvements to the design. Walk-through models were now standard and the spare wheel could be front-mounted on a special bracket to maximize space and retain the flexible layout. A middle seat (with no back) could be set up between the front cab seats, giving extra seating for dining or daytime use. There was also now a side-mounted free-standing tent awning called the Danbury Ridge Tent. For use with the vehicle, one sidewall simply flapped over the roof and the double doors opened directly into the tent. A draught excluder ran between the two wheels and was held in place by a piece of dowelling across the doors. Electric mains hook-up and a refrigerator were also optional extras. Also available was a Webster elevating roof.

The cooker unit was redesigned so that it could be turned in three different directions or sited behind the driver's seat, and the sink unit had extra

The 1966 Danbury Multicar.

A day awning fits over the load doors and the table has folding legs that can be fitted for outdoor use, as shown here.

The Danbury badge is fitted on the engine lid.

The cooker is protected by a hinged top.

The top simply hinges up for use. The table can be seen in position; also note the storage pocket on the rear load door.

The sink unit is normally sited by the door, but can also be sited behind the driver.

Amongst the many layouts was this arrangement to provide a settee or single bed. The sink unit can clearly be seen here.

Reversible cushions are very practical when camping with children.

Optional child's cab bunk.

The rubber dashtop mat is unique to Danbury.

Shelves were fitted on either side of the air vent above the sun visors. They provide handy storage space for maps and the like. These were also Danbury-only features.

At the side of the rear luggage area is a curtained hanging space (wardrobe), next to the spare wheel, with hooks, rail and hangers. A front-mounted spare carrier was available.

drawers fitted. Extra storage in the cab area was achieved through two pockets above the front windscreens and a non-slip rubber surface was fixed to the dashboard top, giving a level area to stand drinks and the like.

Only two Danbury conversions from the sixties are known to have survived – this one, owned by Dave Cantle, was built in 1966 on a Kombi base and finished in Light Grey. The only restoration carried out has been repairs to the bottoms of the loading doors, a new sill and a respray up to the gutter line in 1987. Dave has also given it the very distinctive number plate 8006 VW!

In 1968 the vehicle was shipped to Australia with only 11,868 miles (19,096km) on the clock, then to New Zealand, and finally back to the UK, a year later, in 1969. Service records show it covered 6,500 miles (10,460km) in Australia and 3,500 miles (5,630km) in New Zealand. It regularly entered concours events during the eighties and in 1988 won the coveted SSVC's Van of the Year. The interior is largely original, even down to the red vinyl floor covering, although the carpet was a later addition and carpet on the sides was added in 1987. The table has had trim added and Dave is not sure if it is the original size or not. He says the interior is very basic really and sleeping somewhat of a compromise, being essentially a combination of table and bits of wood between the cupboards with the cushions scattered 'in any order the owner finds comfy!' Although the cushions can be arranged to give many different seating positions Dave is also not sure that all are safe!

1968: THE NEW SHAPE DANBURY

With the advent of the Bay Window generation Danbury went back to the drawing board and for 1969 came up with a very different design aimed at the dual-purpose user, much like the original Multicar, but simply designated 'the Danbury'. Based on either a walk-through Microbus or Kombi, there were now two forward-facing seats as well as a rear bench seat for travelling. Danbury literature of the time emphasized this feature:

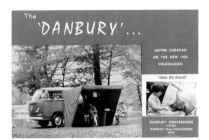

The 1968 brochure cover.

Danbury conversions offer you the best of both worlds. An economical vehicle for everyday use with built-in comfort and unequalled mobility … ideal for town or country. PLUS all the amenities of a luxury caravan. Now the Danbury offers 'FORWARD FACING SEATS' – do away with that crick in the neck – here is the opportunity to go where and when you please in comfort.

The multi-purpose layout was achieved through the movable twin middle seats, which give different seating arrangements depending on use, including a walk-through living area option and an L-shaped day settee reminiscent of the sixties version. For travelling, the two movable seat base units faced forwards. For dining round the table, the seats slid back to the bulkhead and the seat backs slotted upright in a new position. A middle seat could be positioned between the cab walk-through and middle seats to create another long settee facing the rear,

By 1969 adverts for the new Danbury were appearing in the motoring press.

or make a forward-facing cab seat for day use. Curtains and fabrics were usually plain with seat covers matching the body colour (or red for all white Buses).

When the bed was laid down, cushions could be arranged to create a large or small sleeping area. (The Danbury bed is legendary for both its size and intricate layout pattern!) It was also possible to have two single beds. A child's cab stretcher bunk was an optional extra. The cooker/grill was housed under the seat base nearest the sliding door and simply popped up from this housing for use. The inclusion of a sink with drawer and storage unit gave living with the van that little bit of extra versatility. As well as under-seat storage there was a roof locker and a wardrobe sited opposite the spare wheel.

For the first time the Danbury was now readily available with an optional pop-top roof with striped canvas co-ordinating with the main body colour (red stripe for all white vehicles).

1972 Danbury.

For travelling, the seats can be arranged to all face forwards. The table folds flat against the side wall.

For dining, the seats slide back against the bulkhead and the seat backs and cushions are repositioned. The upholstery, curtains and flooring are all original.

The bed is full width and roomy, but is notorious for being complex to lay out.

This period wire dash storage tray is a useful accessory. Note the middle jump seat between the cab seats.

The sink unit is sited at the end of the rear bench.

The pop-up cooker/grill is stored in the base of the single seat behind the front passenger.

The Danbury model featured here was first registered in October 1972. It was used for family holidays until 1986, before being dry-stored with just 32,000 genuine miles (51,490km) on the clock. It stayed like this until 2000, when Robert Sendall stepped in and purchased it as a restoration project. The restoration was done by Robert himself. He then prepped the whole van, before having it repainted in the original colours of Pastel White over Niagara Blue. The interior was then cleaned and refitted, with even the lino flooring being original. The cab is just as impressive and all that needed renewing were small sections of the headliner on the pillars. The engine was rebuilt with unleaded heads, but otherwise remains completely standard. The wheels were fitted with NOS cross-ply tyres on the front, but the rears were good enough to reuse.

The Bus debuted at Vanfest 2003, where it deservedly took First Place in the Bay Window Class and a Best in Show Judges' Choice.

THE DANBURY DELUXE

By the late 1960s Danbury was one of only three officially VW-approved UK converters (along with Dormobile and Devon), and, although they lost this approval when Devon entered into an exclusive contract in 1972, they regained their status in 1977. Although fairly basic, the Danbury layout had worked especially well for those who wanted a vehicle that was a Minibus, occasional load hauler and comfortable Camper. However, in 1977 a new version of the Danbury, now officially VW-approved and with a very different layout, was produced: the Danbury Volkswagen Deluxe.

The elevating roof with two bunks was now standard, as were two opening, sliding rear side windows. A new style of kitchen unit, complete with oven, two-ring hob and grill, was housed in a unit over the rear deck, which slid forwards for use. Seating was arranged in an L shape behind the driver and passenger, and along the side wall. There was also a rear seat in front of the cooker unit when the cooker was not in use (a very similar arrangement to that used on the Viking models). It was also possible to arrange seating round the table on the front of the sliding door. There was a pumped sink unit by the sliding door and a roof locker. All furniture and fittings were in teak, with heat-resistant teak laminate for work and table tops.

Stainless steel cutlery (in its own wallet folder) and melamine crockery place settings for four were also standard equipment, as was a portable cool box. A removable carpet was laid over vinyl flooring and three fluorescent lights (two over the kitchen unit and one over the dinette area) were fitted.

Danbury announced its new conversion with: 'Danbury and Volkswagen – the perfect team – bring you a new luxury conversion – but at a STANDARD price! Danbury has always made its watch words SIMPLICITY and COMFORT; now we add LUXURY and a touch of CLASS.' Only a handful of original condition Danbury Deluxes are known to survive.

Danbury continued to be an approved VW converter during its final years of production until they ceased operating in the late 1980s.

Family camping in 1972 included family pets!

2004: DANBURY IS REBORN!

In 2002 Beetles UK began converting Brazilian Type 2 Buses into Campers and went on to buy up the name Danbury to use for the conversion side of their business.

The new Danbury VW is available in two versions of the famous Bay Window VW Type 2, with all the charm and looks of the original but with the advantages of modern technology. It is powered by an air-cooled 1600cc engine with a multipoint fuel-injection system and a three-way catalytic converter, and is fitted with front disc brakes. Built on the VW production line in Brazil, the 'new' T2 has a few minor differences externally such as a slightly higher roof and raised mouldings on the cab door bottoms. It also has bumpers closer in style to those fitted in the early seventies, minus the built-in step. Other differences include a thick-rimmed rubber steering wheel and the removal of the waist-high front bulkheads, which means that swivelling front seats can easily be fitted. It retains the classic looks of a Bay Window Camper but is brand new and as such comes with a three-year warranty! Two fitted versions are available, as are DIY kits.

The Rio and the Surf

The Rio is the multi-purpose version, often called a 'day van', with removable middle seats. The kitchen, complete with two-burner hob and grill, sink and pumped water and 12V cool box, is sited down the side, with a rock-and-roll (pull-out) bed, dining table and ample storage space. The optional elevating roof allows two hammock bunks to be fitted for more sleeping space.

The Surf is the full-on Camper for those who want a big double bed! The design differs from most VW conversions and allows full access to the well-equipped kitchen, even when the bed is being used. It can seat five people in comfort. The kitchen unit is mounted horizontally across the front of the vehicle, to the rear of the front seats, and incorporates a sealed and vented single-cylinder dedicated gas locker, self-lighting stainless steel hob and grill with matching stainless steel sink and electrically pumped cold water from a removable on-board container, a removable 12V electric cool box (a fitted optional 40ltr chest fridge that can also be used as a deep freeze, is also available). Waste is collected via an external remote socket. There is also a removable free-standing centre-mounted table with detachable leg. The rear metal-framed rock-and-roll rear seat cleverly converts to a flat, large king-size double bed in one simple operation, complete with three lap style rear seat belts. Lighting is via two fluorescent strip lights mounted on the near side and off side, plus chrome swivel ball reading lights mounted at the rear.

Both versions come with an onboard petrol heater and a huge range of options and accessories, including right-hand drive conversion, two-tone paint, heated front and rear screens, fridge freezer, mains hook-up, alloy wheels, bike rack, swivel seats, leather interior and even a TV cabinet with a flat screen TV and DVD player! Camping was never like this in the seventies! For the full story, see www.danburymotorcaravans.co.uk, or telephone Beetles UK on 0870 1202 356, who will happily arrange a test drive and demonstration.

The front cover of the 1976 brochure.

The Deluxe version was introduced in 1977.

Day mode.

Danbury Rio; shown with optional buddy seat and roof rack.

Oatmeal and wood veneer were the style for 1976, although the layout remained the same.

Night mode.

Danbury Surf; shown with optional elevating roof, spare wheel cover and two tone paint.

Dehler is a well-established name both in Germany and the rest of the world. The eighties saw the introduction of the Profi, a luxurious, top of the range conversion, built in Germany by Dehler. It featured Dehler's own design of aerodynamic fixed high roof, complete with opening sunroof. The interior was especially well appointed, with pale shades of laminate and matching upholstery. The flexible seating, with rotating, movable twin forward seats, allowed for forward-facing travel, dinette round a table or a settee under the window layouts, as well as becoming the double bed. A TV was mounted in the roof space above the cab and a bathroom/shower compartment was sited behind the driver. Dehler was amongst the first to recognize the huge potential of the 'Woopi' (well-off older people) market and to design an interior geared to their needs; part of which was a desire to get away from it all – but without roughing it! Around 1997 Dehler ran into financial problems and stopped production of Dehler Campers. Now they are a member of the Neptune group (a Dutch–Canadian group) and back in their original business of making yachts.

The first Devon Brochure was produced in 1958.

Devon produced one of the most famous UK conversions, best known for its high-quality finish and oak woodwork. Devon were one of the very few converters to be officially licensed by VW, which meant that the full VW warranty and after-sales service applied to all new vehicles. Other companies had to provide their own warranty. Devon quickly cornered the market and became the UK's most popular conversion in the sixties and seventies.

1957–67:
THE SPLIT WINDOW YEARS

Getting in on the Leisure Boom:
The Devon Caravette

In 1957 VW Dealers Lisburne Garages of Torquay, in Devon, joined forces with the cabinet makers J.P. White of Sidmouth to produce a motor caravan based on the VW Bus. J.P. White were responsible for the design and construction of the new Campervan, whilst Lisburne Garages were responsible for sales, distribution and after-sales service.

In January 1958 the new Devon Caravette conversion was officially launched, based on the VW Microbus and priced at £897 10s. The conversion was superbly crafted using hand-polished solid light oak. It featured the well-known basic table and bench seating dinette arrangement, which converted to a double bed by dropping the table down between the bench units. Dunlopillo foam of 4in (100mm) thickness and covered with removable, washable covers was used for seating, and curtains on slide

runners were also fitted. The flooring consisted of two-colour (usually black and white) polyfloor tiles laid in a check pattern. To the rear of the loading doors along the side of the rear bench seat was a curved storage cabinet, the top of which hinged up to take a two-burner gas cooker. Extra storage space was through small units with sliding doors on the top of the forward bench seat and behind the rear bulkhead above the engine compartment. This area also doubled as a child's bed. Two Formica-covered tables were supplied, one of which folded down and the other stowed in the roof above the engine compartment when not needed, doubling as a shelf. The interior lighting was augmented with a gas light, with the gas cylinder housed in a special locker beneath the child's bed at the rear when travelling and coupled to an outside point for use (to comply with safety regulations).

A canvas tent awning extension was also available, with or without side flaps (cost ranged from £18 16s to £36 15s) and a roof rack could be fitted for an extra £18. A water carrier and washbasin were also available as extras. The table could be used free standing outside and the 1958 brochure also showed an open storage container fitted to the left loading door. The Caravette conversion was also available based on a Deluxe Microbus at a cost of £1,092 10s. Additionally, for £200, Lisburne Garages also offered to fit out Caravette conversions to privately owned Microbuses, providing they were structurally sound. Interestingly, some of the very first advertisements

The handbuilt, curved side cabinet was testament to the craftsmanship of the early Devons.

Sliding door storage was built into the rear of the bench seat.

All the woodwork has ID numbers stamped in to aid assembly.

for the new Caravette actually depicted a Barndoor Bus.

In October that year the Devon Caravette debuted at the Caravan and Boats Exhibition at Earl's Court. By then, three versions of the Caravette were offered. The Mark I was the budget model, priced at £910, with the same specs as already described, but the Mark II, priced at £930 also featured a water tank with pump tap mounted in a cupboard behind the front bulkhead, hinge-down washing bowl on the loading door, and an Osokool food storage cabinet under the front bench seat. The Mark II version was also available fitted to the Deluxe Microbus for £1,105. The Mark III version was rather different and was geared to a very different market – the commercial traveller.

Devon Mark III

The Mark III conversion was specifically tailored for the 'Gentleman of the Road' and advertised as 'A pleasure to drive – a joy to work with.' As well as a rear bench seat with storage under, another bench ran under the windows and the table was affixed to the front bulkhead so that one could sit on the long bench unit to work or eat. This doubled as a single bed, which could also be made up to form a double bed 'for the family at weekends and holidays'. The unit for the water tank and pump was fitted as per the camping version, but no cool box was

included and there were no door-mounted cupboards. A two-burner cooker was housed in the curved side cabinet and, when in use, the top of the unit detached and was affixed above the cooker across the side window to form a very useful shelf.

Another feature, not found on the camping conversions, was the inclusion of a wooden filing/storage cabinet, which was stored under the open bench seat. An open-fronted hanging wardrobe was sited in the rear. Advertising material extolled the advantages of a mobile office/lounge as perfect for 'entertaining your customer, ideal for writing your report', continuing with 'The Caravette in the Commercial Traveller's model provides adequate accommodation to entertain clients and provides the psychological advantage of playing on your home ground instead of the client's office, some hospitality can sometimes be offered which can make all the difference between the cold shoulder and a cordial reception with beneficial results.' The flexibility to spend as long as needed in one location without the need to book or find accommodation was also a key part of the sales pitch. However, it would seem likely that the market for such a conversion was limited; the model and layout had been discontinued by 1959 and no surviving examples of this layout have been found or recorded.

1960: The New Caravette

In 1959 the cooker had been relocated and mounted in a specially designed cabinet onto the loading door, though it was still stored for travelling in the curved side cabinet. However, in the latter half of 1960 there was a complete redesign, which gave more space and facilities. Unfortunately, the lovely hand-built curved cabinet was dropped in favour of squarer units that were quicker, easier and cheaper to build. The curved units were craftsmanship at its best and are much prized today, if one can be found!

For the 1960 Earl's Court Motor Show J.P. White displayed the revamped Devon Caravette, along with conversions on the Morris J2 and Austin 152 entitled Sleep-A-Kar. Both a standard Microbus and Deluxe Microbus were exhibited but now there was only one style, providing sleeping accommodation for two adults and two children. All the best features of the previous versions were retained, but now the Caravettes all featured an 11gal (50ltr) water tank (sited under the front bench seat) with water supply to the built-in sink by means of a double-action rocker pump, a 3ft (0.9m) wardrobe with mirror, a combined crockery and cutlery unit with flap-down doors to give wipe-clean worktops and fitted with melamine crockery and cutlery for four, a built-in magazine rack, two small cupboards fitted to the

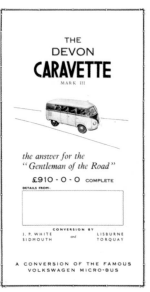

HOME COOKING—
a compact and simple to operate built-in cooker ensures good meals

THE LOUNGE AND OFFICE—
neat, compact and comfortable, perfect for entertaining your customer, ideal for writing your report

SETTLED FOR THE NIGHT—
and who could fail to sleep well in this luxurious single bed, with deep 4in. foam mattresses

A double bed for the family at the weekend and holidays

Adequate locker space and a filing cabinet is provided for your records

The Caravette Traveller was aimed specifically at the commercial traveller; note the bulkhead-mounted table, L-shaped seating, cooker shelf and wooden filing cabinet.

For 1960 a flap shelf was fitted to the front load door.

The cooker is mounted in a cabinet on the rear load door.

The curved cabinet was retained until late 1960. Note the gas light.

rear roof corners, contemporary table legs for both tables, an improved side awning and slightly greater length for the child's bunk. The Osokool unit was replaced with an Easicool version still sited in the shortened front bench unit to allow for the siting of the wardrobe on the bulkhead. The cooker cupboard on the rear loading door now could store the cooker when not in use and the curved cupboard unit became a sink unit with pump tap, angled not curved with black Formica faced doors and sink worktop. The gas bottle was now stored in the engine compartment and coupled to fitting points for use.

For 1961 the cooker cupboard was redesigned to accommodate a new cooker with bigger burners and a grill.

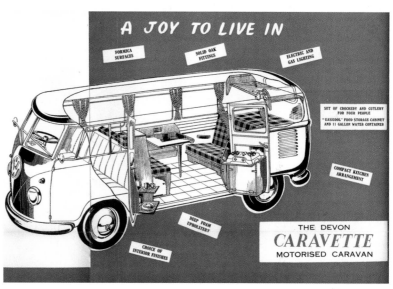

This cutaway drawing shows the new layout for 1961.

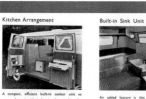

The 1961 Caravettes changed the curved cabinet for a sink unit with Formica doors and pump tap and a crockery cupboard was fitted to the front load door. These were the only Devon models to feature a fitted sink unit.

This fully original 1961 Deluxe is owned by Ritchie King.

The new style cooker/grill, with windshield, is housed in a new style of cabinet.

Cushions are still in the original fabric. Note the magazine rack and ashtray.

A passenger headrest, in matching fabric, was standard on the Deluxe conversions.

The cooker cabinet is mounted on the load doors. The woodwork on this model is finished in mahogany.

1962: The Devonette – Budget Camping with Versatility

In 1962 Devon reintroduced a budget version entitled the Devonette. Being based on the Kombi instead of the Microbus, the vehicle was single colour, although two-tone paint was available for an extra £15. The emphasis was on basic camping and a bigger space. The woodwork in the Devonette was finished in dark mahogany, but light oak finish was available for an additional £6 10s and the flooring was single-colour Polyfloor tiles. The cooker was a basic two-burner, initially mounted for use

The Devonette, introduced in 1962, was the budget model, with a large wardrobe against the front bulkhead, just inside the load door.

on the front loading door unit but later on the rear one. Three 2gal (9ltr) water containers and a plastic washing-up bowl were supplied and there was only one table, though a wardrobe (sited by the load door on the bulkhead) and Easicool units were retained. As there was less furniture, the amount of floor space in the load area was bigger than in the Caravette. With a price of £819 10s it came in at nearly £150 cheaper than the Caravette version, making it a more affordable option.

1962: The Gentlux Elevating Roof

The 1962 Caravette models were essentially the same as before, except the side awning was now standard equipment, but one innovation offered as an extra for both the Devonette and Caravette, priced at £65, was Devon's own designed fibre-glass elevating roof, called the Gentlux Elevating Roof giving 6ft 6in (2m) standing room. The publicity material of the time stated, 'The roof is particularly suitable for the Devonette as in

this conversion the large area of floor space can be utilised to the full.' This was a response to the newly launched Dormobile conversion, which was the first full-size elevating roof conversion on a VW Camper. The Gentlux was a small pop-top roof with a fitted skylight. Very few survive today as it was discontinued the following year in favour of the Martin Walter version.

One improvement to the Caravette was to be able to cook inside by having an alternative arrangement that allowed the cooker to detach from the door and be positioned in alternative slots against the tall locker/wardrobe cabinet. With the cooker in this position the flexible gas pipe plugged into a second gas tap beside the locker so that the pipe did not trail across the open doors. In addition to the underfloor 11gal water tank a 2gal water container for drinking water was also supplied. The old-fashioned gas light was replaced by a modern fluorescent strip light mounted centrally opposite the loading doors. The Deluxe Microbus version was also available in mahogany wood at no extra cost.

Flooring, fabrics and curtains are in immaculate, original condition on this 1962 Caravette. The magazine rack can be seen under the table.

The door-mounted crockery cupboard.

The cooker was mounted on the rear load door, but could also be positioned against the wardrobe locker for inside use.

A typical Devon feature was the inclusion of extra storage in the bench seat backs. The gas point for the inside cooker is just visible centre left.

Table and bed boards are stowed in the roof at the rear.

Built-in gas lines and fitting points were provided.

This original 1962 interior, fitted to a Samba, shows the new style of cooker and cabinet.

The 1962/3 models were the only ones to feature a fitted sink and swivel action pump tap.

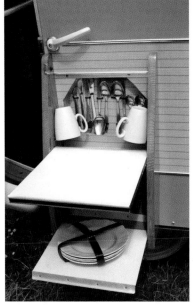

The door-mounted crockery cabinet was a useful addition.

A passenger headrest was optional, but standard on Deluxe conversions. Note the gas point to allow the cooker to be resited for indoor use.

The new 1964 Caravette models were available from late 1963.

The 1963/64 Devonette had the cooker sited at the end of the bench.

The cooker, with windshield, and a pump tap were sited at the end of the rear bench, and a vanity unit with washing bowl was fitted to the rear load door.

For 1964 the Dormobile roof and drive-away awning became available.

The cooker was demountable for outside use, and water containers were stored under the front bench.

1963: More Sleeping and Standing Space

For 1963 both the Devonette and the Caravette were available on either a Microbus or Kombi base and it was also possible to specify two-tone paint for the Kombi model. The Gentlux elevating roof option was replaced with the newly available side-hinged Martin Walter elevating roof option, with roof windows, designed and supplied by Dormobile. This unit could also have optional bunks fitted, thus dramatically increasing sleeping potential. Standing height was now 6ft 6in, making movement much easier and reducing backache!

For the Caravette version the sink unit was discontinued and the cooker was now sited in the side cabinet, complete with all-round heat/weather shield and warming rack. Alternatively, the whole cooking unit could be transferred outside, mounted on legs to use as a camp kitchen under the free-standing awning. A new cabinet with matching mirror and plastic bowl was fitted to the rear loading door, whilst a redesigned cabinet on the front loading door housed the supplied crockery and cutlery. Water was dispensed from a 7.5gal (34ltr) tank via a swivel action pump. Vinyl floor tiles, Doracour zip covers on the foam seating and melamine-topped

tables were refinements in keeping with the modern materials now available. The small roof corner cupboards were no longer standard fitting.

The 1963 Devonette now featured a two-burner cooker complete with grill, which was also demountable for outside use. Water was stored in three 2gal polythene containers, which were carried under the front bench seat (where the Easicool unit was sited in the Caravette). Other features not found in the Devonette included the side awning, load door cabinets, rear drawer units, curtains for the cab area, crockery and cutlery, a single table instead of two tables, a fluorescent strip light and the Easicool fridge. Whilst the Caravette retained hand-polished oak woodwork the Devonette woodwork was just finished in natural oak. However, any of these standard Caravette features could be ordered as add-on extras for the Devonette. Other extras included: factory sliding sunroof, two-tone paint (for the Kombi), cab bunk, Devon side step and a portable toilet.

Also available this year was a newly designed Devon Drive Away Frame Tent, made by S.T. Harrison of Bristol, which meant that the vehicle could drive off leaving the tent and equipment behind for the day. The newly introduced 1500cc engine was also available at an extra charge.

1965: The Torvette

At the Earl's Court Motor Show In October 1965 Devon introduced a slightly revamped version of the Devonette, and renamed it the Torvette. It was based on the Kombi, so trim was more basic, and, apart from its lower price, the appeal continued to be the adaptable layout with the potential for large floor space enabling the vehicle to be used as load hauler, people carrier and family Camper. The interior hardly differed from the refinements introduced to the Devonette back in 1963, except that the flap-down shelf for the washing bowl on the right loading door increased in size and an Easicool unit was now fitted at the end of the rear bench seat. There was also a cupboard unit with two compartments on the rear compartment wall opposite the slide-down door wardrobe and a roof cupboard across the whole rear section.

The Caravette remained essentially the same as previously except that Gaydon melamine crockery consisting of four beakers, plates and fruit plates was standard and the cutlery set now included a bread knife! The rear cupboard opposite the wardrobe had a single door and the compartment was tall enough to carry bottles securely held in place with elastic straps.

The Torvette Spaceway has two single seats either side of the gangway.

The cooker is fitted against the front bulkhead behind the single seat back. The cooker folds out, complete with windshield, for use.

Cushion covers and curtains are all original. Note the roof cabinet, only fitted to Torvettes.

Twin cushions make up the rear bench back. The cooker cabinet is visible behind the single seat.

Two rear drawers carry the spare wheel and awning; the wardrobe is sited at the side.

Extra storage is provided behind the other single seat.

1966: The Spaceway Versions

For 1966 Devon introduced a walk-through version called the Spaceway, which was available for both the Caravette and the Torvette models, and which allowed the cab and living areas to be connected. This meant a redesign of the interior to accommodate the lack of a bulkhead. The front bench seat now became a single seat with storage locker underneath and the rear cushion could be positioned against the bulkhead or the side wall for travelling or dining. The Caravette featured a new swing-out cupboard unit for the cooker/water pump which was located on the other side of the gangway against the bulkhead behind the front passenger seat. The unit housed a two-burner cooker and grill, and was complete with fold-up protective housing with a warming rack. The front folded down to make a useful standing area for the grill pan or utensils and there was a small cutlery drawer on the left under the cooker. Under that was a small cupboard to house the gas bottle. To the right was a larger height cupboard for storing the 7.5gal water tank and at the right side of the unit was the water pump compartment, also with a flap-down side. A small bolt on the rear bottom right corner secured the unit in position when inside the vehicle. The whole unit was hinged down the left side and attached to the side wall enabling it to swing-out, when both loading doors were open, for outside cooking. The cupboard doors were all wipe-clean black melamine and the insides were also faced with melamine to match the table top. To accommodate this unit, the front loading door no longer had a crockery cupboard mounted on it.

The Easicool larder fridge was located at the end of the rear bench seat and the seat above the unit slid out on runners to give the cook somewhere to sit and watch the kettle boil or make the toast in comfort when cooking inside!

The compartment above the engine had space for a water container on the left, a unit with two larger pull-out drawers (which could also be accessed from above) and a storage area with a flap-down door on the right. This was where the awning was carried; the spare wheel was stored in the left drawer.

A side awning was standard for both models; side sheets and valence were add-on options to make a fully weatherproof tent awning. The large Devon Drive Away Frame Tent was also still available, and a matching toilet tent now could be ordered! Bunks for the elevating roof and a child's bunk for the front cab were also optional extras. Devon also made and fitted a slide-out step for under the load doors and the cranked gear extension lever (a boon for drivers with short reach!).

The Torvette and Caravette, in fixed or elevating roof, walk-through or bulkhead models were the best-selling UK conversions, but with the advent of the new Bay Window Model in August 1967, Devon had to return to the drawing board and remodel the interior to meet demands for more luxury in the motor caravan markets.

This 1967 Devon Spaceway has been owned by David and Cee Eccles since 1978.

The cabinet is original but new handles, cooker and heat-shield have been fitted.

Dinette mode. The mirror is original Devon equipment.

Original curtains and the Caravette style of rear cabinet can be seen in this view.

One arrangement makes a single bed or day settee under the windows.

The walk-through arrangement to connect cab and living space is both practical and versatile.

The Caravette did not have a roof locker as standard, though one could be specified.

The 1967 Torvette bulkhead model. Note the bulkhead storage and shelf. Cushions and curtains are original, but trim panels and fabric screen for the water containers are updates.

A 1966 Torvette interior. Floor tiles and trim panels are original, but the original green/black fleck fabric has been replaced with a modern fabric.

Although a rock-and-roll bed has been fitted, the original cushions have been retained.

The cooker housing is original but the original cooker is missing and has been replaced with a retro style later unit.

The cooker is sited above the cool box in bulkhead Torvettes, but has legs for outside use.

Dinette mode.

The roof locker is a Torvette-only feature.

The seat base above the cool box slides out to make an extra seat for dining or cooking inside (Caravettes had this feature as well).

The rear cabinet in Torvettes has two sections.

The maker's plate is fixed on the tailgate.

1968–79: THE BAY WINDOW YEARS

Of Caravettes, Torvettes, Eurovettes, Moonrakers, Sunlanders, Devonettes and Sundowners!

Devon continued with their range of fully equipped Camper and more basic budget model, on both Kombi and Microbus bases, carrying the names Caravette and Torvette respectively. However, a brand new design, called the Eurovette, was now introduced as the top of the range model, which set new standards in design and equipment. Walk-through models were now standard for all conversions and the Martin Walter elevating roofs were replaced with Devon's own pop-top roof.

In late 1970 Devon launched their most famous conversion – the Moonraker, which showed a complete makeover and redesign of the camping interior, and combined the Caravette and Eurovette specs. The budget model, the Torvette, was replaced by the Sunlander, but during 1971 this too was revamped and the name Devonette was resurrected to replace the Sunlander.

Devon had been one of only three UK companies officially approved as VW camping converters – the other two being Danbury and Dormobile. However, in 1972 they pulled off an exclusive rights deal whereby they, as officially VW approved, would retail their Buses through the dealer network and have full VW warranty and service. The model chosen was based on the Devonette's multi-purpose approach combined with the camping/people carrier use, and launched in 1972 as the new VW Devon Caravette. VW UK sales brochures promoted the Westfalia Continental as the purpose-built Camper and focused on the versatility of the Devon Caravette in their descriptions and pictures.

During the 1970s Devon experimented with various design and interior layout changes, resurrecting the name Eurovette for their top of the range conversion in 1973. In 1976 The Caravette was renamed Devonette once more and, interestingly, Devon brochures of the time also carried information on the Continental, 'imported from West Germany' (no mention of Westfalia), which they could supply. In 1978 the special arrangement with VW ceased and Devon launched a new range, which included non-VW conversions. They also introduced a completely re-designed Moonraker and replaced the Devonette with the Sundowner. The Moonraker continued to be Devon's most popular and well-designed camping unit and it deservedly won awards when relaunched.

1968–70: The Torvette, Caravette and Eurovette

The Devon range expanded in 1968 with the introduction of the new top of the range Eurovette. The new shape and dimensions of the Bay Window model meant a redesign for all models in terms of both layout and equip-ment, though higher spec Eurovette standard equipment such as the sink could be ordered as an option for the other models.

The Torvette was based on the Kombi whilst the Caravette and Eurovette were based on the new luxurious Deluxe version of the Samba, called the Clipper. All three models had cooker, water storage and built-in food cooler, a pull-out style double bed, wardrobe with shoe compartment, roof locker and rear compartment drawers, which were also accessible through the back of the rear bench seat. Cabinets were finished in light oak, flooring was

Armstrong relief textured tiles, and cushions were now reversible with vinyl on one side and Duracour fabric on the reverse. A large sun awning (with two detachable sides for the Eurovette) was also standard and the new models were all available with the optional new style Devon pop-top roof.

Additional standard features on the Caravette and Eurovette included a 7gal (32ltr) plastic water tank with Whale pump, plus fluorescent lighting. The Eurovette featured as standard a child's cab hammock bunk, melamine crockery and stainless steel cutlery set for four persons, built-in sink unit (optional on the Caravette, which had a food storage compartment as standard in place of the sink), and a built-in oven with the two-burner cooker/grill that was demountable for outside use. The Dudley cooker on the Caravette and Eurovette had a fold-up wind/heat shield and plate-warming rack. A special Devon passenger head-rest in matching fabric was also standard and the table featured a hinged extension flap. These were available as optional extras for the other models.

The wardrobe was sited behind the driver's side passenger seat, with a hinged box seat in front of it, and a similar unit by the loading doors had a food storage cupboard, sliding doors to the cool box, and a water tank (if fitted) at the bottom with a flap-down door. Because of the extra space taken up with the sink and cooker/oven, the Eurovette did not have a box seat in

front of this unit, whereas the Caravette did. The cooker and sink (or food storage unit) were sited by the rear seat inside the sliding door. The Caravette roof locker had two doors, the Eurovette just one. The bed was a pull-out affair with a sliding base, which extended into the area above the engine and had screw-on legs on the front end. The bed could also be laid down between the seats as on the Splitty versions. It was possible to order a Eurovette without the oven unit or sink, in which case the Caravette style cooker with a pump tap unit was sited at the end of the bench seat, allowing more floor space. The Torvette was fairly basic, with just a cooker behind the passenger seat and a cool box under the full width rear seat.

The 1970 Caravettes sported a circular brass badge on the rear hatch, which was replaced by stickers for 1971 onwards.

This 1968 Eurovette has been with the Ward family since new. It has been meticulously cared for and has fewer than 43,000 miles (69,190km) on the clock! The 1968 Eurovette set new standards and even featured an oven; this example is in immaculate condition. The Bus originally was a fixed-roof model, but in 1975 the owners took it back to the Devon works to have an elevating roof and bunks fitted. However, the bunks have never been slept in! Very few of these early Eurovettes survive and certainly none is in this original, unrestored condition.

1968 Eurovette.

The new style of passenger head restraint was standard on the Eurovette.

The kitchen and washing facilities are sited on the nearside. The combined oven/hob unit (with serious heat and windshield and plate-warming rack) actually runs in front of the sliding door, but is demountable for outside use. Even the washing bowl was colour co-ordinated!

There are Devon badges on the tailgate and side window.

With the table flap down, access to the rear from the cab is easy. Note the roof locker.

The wardrobe and other storage are behind the single seat. Note the reversible cushions – cloth one side and wipe-clean vinyl on the reverse.

The pull-out high bed is similar in style to the Moonraker, which replaced the Eurovette in 1970.

The unit just inside the sliding door houses the larder, cool box and water tank. The cutlery in its own wallet is stored in the bottom section and secured to the door with press studs.

An extension flap on the table makes for easy access round the cooker/oven unit to the dining/seating area.

The rear drawers run full length and can be accessed from inside or outside.

1970 Caravette.

Twin locker doors access the roof storage.

Shallow pull-out drawers can also be accessed from inside.

The cooker and pump tap is sited in a unit by the end of the rear bench.

Reversible cushions were standard. Note the filler neck for the water tank in the larder unit.

The seat base detaches to access a cool box, larder and water tank.

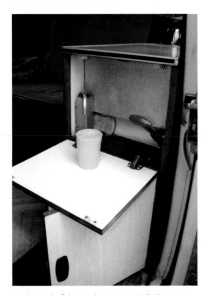

At the end of the cooker unit is a Whale pump and tap, with storage for the gas bottle under.

The cooker has an excellent heat shield and a useful warming rack.

This 1970 Caravette interior was in a Bus bought from new but subsequently refitted into a 1972 Bus when the 1970 one became too expensive to repair. The white table is original to this particular interior because the wife could not stand the garish orange and asked Devon to substitute it! It underwent some minor modifications when being refitted, most notably the loss of the wardrobe cabinet behind the single seat, which was also reduced in height.

1970: The Moonraker and the Sunlander

By 1970 Devon had very clearly established that there were two distinct markets – the dedicated Camper, who wanted to combine freedom to travel with home comforts, and those who wanted versatility from the vehicle, so that it could serve as a people carrier (especially for families) and also double as a load hauler or basic Campervan. In many respects this latter approach was a development of the Camping Box fitted to a Kombi, pioneered by Westfalia. A fast expanding leisure market led to the development of Devon's most popular conversion – the Moonraker, which became their new superior camping conversion from late 1970. The Moonraker interior certainly lived up to its claim to be 'the ultimate in luxury'. An extra cab seat could be made up in the space between the front cab seats and the seat behind the driver was fitted with sliders, allowing it to be used in forward- or rearward-facing position. Two pull-out drawers over the engine compartment could be accessed from the rear or via the rear bench seat; they were used to make the high position bed base, either as single or double. Additionally, or alternatively, the bed could be made up between the bench seats.

A wardrobe was fitted at the rear opposite the spare wheel. A unit at the side of the rear bench seat housed a sink, 6gal (27ltr) water tank with pump and tap, and a plastic lined crockery cupboard, all accessed from top-hinged worktops. Under the sink was a small Easicool cool box. The cooker was Devon's unique swing-out unit, very similar to that used on the earlier Spaceway conversions but minus the water pump. The roof cupboard now housed a two-speed electric fresh air fan, with outlet grille in the floor of the cupboard and plastic cap on the roof, acting as both extractor or cooler. The two-speed switch was mounted at the side of the rear cabinet. Optional extras for both models included: elevating roof with two bunks; a child's hammock bunk for the cab; side awning; tent awning; crockery and cutlery sets; cab centre seat; headrests; large and small roof racks; side step; fly screens; a small outside table; and factory-fitted electric fans. Awnings were still attached to a channel fixed to the roof.

Dave White owns this lovely 1972 Moonraker.

Woodwork is polished oak with white melamine-faced doors.

The patent Devon swing-out cooker can be used inside …

… or rotated for outside use.

When the cooker is used outside a handy table can be fixed behind it against the bulkhead.

The Moonraker featured a new style of sink unit, with Whale pump and storage at the side.

The deep stainless steel sink is a modern-looking design.

The 1971 Moonraker's sleeping arrangements can be seen in these pictures.

The single seat behind the driver can be reversed to face forwards by sliding the base back and slotting the backrest in the other side.

To form the single bed at the lower level, the backrest from the single seat is used, laid between the seat base and the rear seat.

Seat cushions are then used to form the mattress.

The higher level bed uses the luggage area platform and one or two table tops, and is formed firstly by pulling the drawers out about 6in, then dropping the top part of the rear seat backrest down.

The table tops fit into a channel on the backrest, and are supported at the other end by the legs provided. One table top forms a single bed; both table tops are used to form the double.

Bunk ready for use. When not in use, they are neatly stored with a press-stud vinyl cover.

The Sunlander was designed to be a people carrier and basic Camper. Instead of a swing-out cooker, an extra sliding seat was positioned behind the front passenger seat. The front seats were cleverly designed to allow them to face forwards for travelling, or rearwards for dining/living. There was no sink and the cooker was a small flap-down unit, sited at the end of the rear bench seat (where the sink unit was for the Moonraker). A shelf (stored by the spare wheel) was fitted into a channel below the cooker, which had a vinyl cover when not in use. The gas cylinder was stored in the engine compartment along with space to carry 'a standard one gallon container' (the thought of a gas bottle and petrol in a can in the engine compartment is a bit scary!). Food storage in the Sunlander was in special plastic-lined, insulated compartments at either end of the rear seat locker, and water was carried in three 2gal (9ltr) plastic carriers under the sliding seat base. The roof cupboard two-way fan was standard, as for the Moonraker, but upholstery and cushions were only available in orangey brown, whatever the exterior colour of the Bus.

When not in use the cooker folds up; it is protected by a vinyl cover.

The conversion offered comfortable, roomy seating. Note the integral armrests.

The seats have reversible backs, allowing seats to be positioned for either travel or dining.

The cooker sits on a shelf, which is stored in the rear when not in use.

A two-way fan/extractor is housed in the upper storage cupboard.

Conversion badges showing the model are usually found on the dashboard.

Travelling mode. The worn upholstery has been replaced to harmonize with the Bus colours.

The fresh air fan intake/outlet is mounted on the roof.

This 1971 Sunlander is owned by Carl Witham and is the only one of two known still to have all its original fittings. The Sunlander was designed as a multi-purpose vehicle and, as it was only made for one year, is a rarely seen conversion.

A plastic liner under the rear seat makes a simple cool box.

Dining mode.

1972 Devonette.

The bed is made up by repositioning the single seats and laying out the back boards.

Travel mode. The cooker can be seen folded against the front bulkhead.

The cooker has no grill and the housing folds up onto legs for use.

Room with a view!

1971: The Devonette is Back!

The 1972 models, displayed in October 1971, showed a clearer separation between camping and multi-purpose use – the Moonraker's basic spec was improved whilst the Sunlander became the Devonette.

The Devonette was described as having 'all the advantages of an estate car for travelling PLUS the sleeping, cooking, dining and storage facilities of a real motor caravan', whilst the Moonraker was, 'equally spacious but with many additional refinements for the discriminating motor caravanner, offering the ultimate in luxury'. Both were available on either a Kombi or Microbus base, with the options of Devon's own design of pop-top elevating roof and the free-standing Devon Motent, which now used plastic channelling to attach to the gutter.

In many respects, the models were a refinement on the previous year's models. Both conversions were still finished in light oak for the cabinet works, and, for the Moonraker, white-faced melamine doors and drawer fronts. The roof locker above the engine compartment on the Moonraker was still accessed by twin doors with a two-way fresh air fan to avoid condensation; the Devonette's roof locker space had no door or fan. Whilst the Moonraker kept a swing-out cooker/grill cupboard and sink unit, the Devonette featured a new style of cooker, with only two burners, fixed to the bulkhead behind the front passenger seat, which flapped down for use and gave more seating space on the rear bench seat, something the Sunlander had lacked. The Devonette also had a double sliding front seat, which could be arranged to face forwards or backwards, depending on required use.

The Devonette was the more basic of Devon's range, but it featured a multi-purpose layout, achieved through the movable twin middle seats that gave different seating arrangements depending on use, including a 'walk-through' living area option. This 1972 model had only two previous owners before being purchased by Shaun Mitchell. It needed quite extensive work to the body, before being taken completely back to bare metal and resprayed in the original colours of Niagara Blue and Pastel White. The interior was then restored and refitted with new carpet and upholstery. All the work was done by Shaun and his dad and the van was completed in time for the Volksworld Show 2002, where it took a trophy for 'Best Stock Type 2' – the ultimate accolade.

Standard fittings for the Moonraker, which were available as optional extras for the Devonette, included fluorescent lighting, a cab centre seat/locker, melamine crockery, stainless steel cutlery, electric extractor fan and a child's cushion bed. Other extras that could be specified for either model included: gas cylinder and regulator; a sliding sunroof for the cab; a retractable side step (Devon's own design as opposed the VW option); a cab hammock bunk; headrests; cab seat covers; fire extinguisher;

fly screens; portable refrigerator; portable Elsan toilet; toilet tent; roof rack; roof-mounted spare wheel carrier and cover; and mains power intake.

A circular Devon sticker naming the actual conversion (Moonraker, Devonette and so on) was still located on the dash under the radio and another sticker was positioned in the middle of the front grille.

The Kombi models were single colour, initially in Pastel White, Neptune Blue or Chianti Red, whilst the Microbus was finished in Pastel White or Pastel White over Niagra Blue, Sierra Yellow or Chianti Red. For the Moonraker curtains and coverings were matched so that all-white Buses had red curtains, oatmeal seat-coverings and beige flooring; blue versions had blue curtains, blue fabric and grey flooring; red Buses had red curtains and covers with grey flooring (except the Kombi version, which had beige flooring); and yellow versions featured gold curtains and seat coverings with grey flooring. The Devonette, however, was finished with yellow curtains, beige floor and seat coverings whatever the exterior colour ordered.

1972: The Devon VW Caravette

The Devon VW Caravette was officially and exclusively licensed by VW from 1972 and was available from VW dealerships as one of the two authorized VW Camper conversions carrying full VW warranty. VW adopted the same approach as Devon for its choice of models – the Devon Caravette was marketed for its versatility and the Westfalia Continental for its purpose-built camping conversion (interestingly, VW brochures of the time made no mention of the names of the converters, simply adopting the names Caravette and Continental). Both models were based on the Microbus body. A 1972 brochure summed up the appeal of the Caravette:

> Our Camper is not just a Camper. It's whatever you want it to be. A roomy estate car or a Minibus, a runabout for picking up the kids or the shopping. You might think that is enough for any car, not so with this one. When other cars finish this VW begins.

Images from the 1972 Brochure showing layouts and use.

It can be your English country cottage or your villa in some sun drenched foreign part. And unlike any cottage or villa you can pack up and go, anywhere you like, whenever you like. A VW Camper is built to work hard and play hard – taking the children to school or play, for going fishing or to the races, collecting gardening materials – in fact any of the 1001 uses that our estate car has been designed to do. And after your motor caravan has spent the day working hard, it too likes the special evening out. To the theatre, the ballet or the opera and perhaps, afterwards, an extra special candlelit dinner. Truly a car for all occasions.

No mention of surfers or the alternative culture there!

The seating could be arranged to give eight forward-facing seats or as a dinette round the table. The cushions were covered with a distinctive oatmeal and brown check with complementary striped curtains. A side unit at the end of the rear bench seat housed a stainless steel cooker with two burners and a grill, and a stainless steel washbasin with small draining board. An insulated cool box was fitted at the end of this unit by the sliding door. Water was stored in the compartment beneath the forward-facing bench seat. Storage space was in the wardrobe opposite the spare wheel, a roof locker and beneath the seat units. Washable vinyl floor covering and padded washable fabric on the panels were used to make the interior easy to keep clean. Until October 1972 the woodwork was hand-finished in light oak, but from thence wood laminate or 'quarter cut English oak, satin finished using special melamine polish', was used.

Optional extras included elevating roof, cab hammock bunk, fly screens, portable refrigerator, child's bed cushion, spare wheel cover and fluorescent lighting. It was also now possible to specify the 1700cc engine or automatic transmission.

The Caravette was sold for its multi-purpose approach, and its camping facilities were superior to the Devonette. It was marketed through VAG dealerships, but could also be ordered direct from Devon. The Bus featured here is a 1973 Devon Caravette, owned by Graham Booth, that has had an original 1972 Caravette interior fitted, which means that the woodwork is solid oak, not laminate finish. The cushions, curtains and worktops are all original. The distinctive Devon pop top can clearly be seen.

1973 Caravette, with 1972 Caravette wood interior.

The small table has been specially built to match; although not original it blends perfectly and makes an ideal coffee table.

The bed uses seat base and boards.

For travelling, seats faced forwards. The sink/cooker/cool box is sited at the side of the rear bench.

Seating is arranged dinette style for eating.

The wardrobe is sited in the rear.

A worktop hinges back to reveal a stainless steel cooker and sink with drainer.

The lined cool box has compartments in the door for extra storage of bottles and so on.

Seat backs can be repositioned for forwards or rear-facing use.

The woodwork on 1972 models was still in oak.

The Mid-Seventies

The mid-1970s saw Devon changing around names and specifications. The 1974 models, available from late 1973, saw the introduction of a new top of the range model called the Eurovette, based on the Microbus, with the Caravette name still used for the multi-purpose version, aptly based on the Kombi model; both were available from VW dealers. As such, Eurovettes were two-tone and Caravettes single colour (unless two-tone paint was specially ordered). Elevating roof canvases for both models were co-ordinated to the colour of the van, with brown/orange/white and green/blue/white being the most common. In 1976 the Caravette was renamed as the Devonette.

The Eurovette

The Eurovette was the full camping spec version with all the features and options always associated with the top of the range model. New features included a slimline swing-out cooker (now advertised as a Devon patented design), which swung through 90 degrees or could be removed and used outside, an electric water pump operated from the cab, a louvred window on the driver's side, fluorescent lighting as standard, and a pull-out bed instead of rearranging seats and boards. The unit at the end of the rear bench seat was made bigger, allowing the cool box space to be increased, as was sink and draining capacity and storage space. The unit housed a 1gal (4.5ltr) plastic carrier, 5gal (23ltr) water tank, stainless steel sink and drainer, and a wire crockery basket. For the first time, electric power (with switch in the cab) pumped the water. The larger cool box had a holder for milk bottles as well as a storage rack.

A wardrobe/hanging space was fitted directly behind the front bench seat and a cab seat box could be positioned between the cab seats to face forwards (when stationary) or backwards for dining and which folded up when not in use. There were also additional legs for the table to be used outside (stored by the spare wheel beneath the housing of the first-aid kit). It was also possible to

make an additional table behind the cooker when swung out by screwing a leg into the detachable cooker lid.

The 1973 Eurovette cabinets and surfaces were finished in white and yellow laminate, but from 1976 dark rosewood laminate was used. This was coupled with orange and brown diamond pattern lino, yellow, orange and brown floral Sanderson print curtains and orange and brown checked upholstery! Whilst the Kombi continued to be the most common base model a Panel Van conversion was also now available, offering less trim and a cheaper price; the side windows Devon installed in this version were smaller than the VW factory-fitted versions.

The Caravette/Devonette

The layout remained essentially the same as previous Devonettes and VW Devon Caravettes, except that the Caravette now also featured the Devon swing-out cooker. The front bench seat could still face front or back and the wardrobe was sited opposite the spare wheel. The bed still required the front seat to be laid down and cushions positioned on top.

For 1976 this model was redesignated as the Devonette. A removable cool box was added under the rear bench seat and fluorescent lighting and a louvred window became standard. The pull-out bed was also now adopted as standard for the model. A washing-up bowl and 2gal water container were also supplied.

The wood laminate was light oak finish with cupboard doors faced in white melamine. Work surfaces and table tops were orange, and orange and brown curtaining and fabrics in various lurid patterns predominated throughout the interior!

1978: The Devon 21

In 1978, to celebrate Jubilee Year and Devon's twenty-first birthday, a very special limited edition of the Eurovette was produced. Named the 'Devon 21', only fifty were made and very few survive in original condition. Based on the Kombi, but finished in Export colours of Oceanic Blue and White, the interior and upholstery were trimmed in complementary blue and white with a few special refinements. The front cab featured a glove box, a vanity mirror on the passenger sun visor, and a passenger seat with full rake/height reach adjustment. The headlining was 'superior quality cloth' and the door trim panels were black with padded armrests. The seats were black woven plastic leatherette.

In the 'living' area there were adjustable fresh air vents, an ashtray on the offside trim panel behind the driver, a grab handle on the left side of the sliding door opening and the spare wheel had a black plastic cover. All rear trim panels were finished in black vinyl with chrome strips, and around the window areas were finished in white patterned cloth.

The interior conversion was the same as the standard Eurovette layout, but all work surfaces and cupboard doors were of blue melamine with all other furniture panel surfaces in white melamine. The upholstery was in blue check with blue edges and a reverse side and the curtains were matched. The flooring was blue patterned vinyl with a removable blue/black carpet. The blue and white striped elevating roof canvas was also matched to the exterior and interior colour scheme. Also included as standard were a roof rack, fire extinguisher and a twenty-piece blue and white melamine crockery set.

Only fifty of these special edition Eurovettes were produced. The colour makes it stand out at any show!

Although no longer made, the Eurovette layout was adopted for this special edition.

The cooker can be used inside, or rotated out to use with an awning (in good weather!).

Cupboard doors, tables and worktops are finished in pale blue, with white cabinets.

The rear deck was left clear, apart from the spare wheel.

The sink unit is sited by the sliding door at the end of the rear bench.

As well as being finished in Oceanic Blue (a US Export colour), they carried distinctive Devon 21 logos on each cab door.

1978: The New Moonraker and Sundowner Models

'Not so much a vehicle ... more a way of life!' This was the slogan used to launch Devon's new revamped models – this time sporting the well-known name of Moonraker for the full-on Camper and the new name of Sundowner for the multi-purpose Camper. Furniture on both models was chipboard covered with beige-yellow melamine with brown plastic finger pulls and edging and brown worktops. Both models included all the well-known Devon features and the new Sundowner was the best-equipped multi-purpose Camper Devon had produced.

Another innovation for these models was the new Devon Double Top elevating roof. This ran the full length of the roof and was side hinged – much like the old Martin Walter versions. Gas-filled struts made raising the roof easy and the increased sleeping space was substantial – two solid base bed sections could be slid together to provide a 6ft by 3ft 9in (1.8m by 1.1m) double bed or two single children's berths.

The entire Double Top interior and undersides of the bed units were lined with carpet style material and the canvas skirt was colour coded to complement the vehicle colour. The side panels for both models were covered in carpet style trim to window level and a removable brown carpet was fitted to all floor areas including the cab and walk-through sections. Under the carpet was laid patterned vinyl floor covering (brown and cream for the Moonraker and brown and beige for the Sundowner).

To create more space the spare wheel was relocated to a mounting bracket fitted to a hinged cradle and fixed externally above the rear bumper, and fitted with a black vinyl cover. A double louvred window continued to be fitted to the offside front. Optional extras included the standard elevating pop-top roof as well as the new Devon Double Top, refrigerator (gas or 240V) and 240V mains hook-up (Moonraker only), side step and cab hammock bunk. The Sundowner could also have matching cab seat covers. The 2ltr engine, with brake servo and radial tyres, was also available as an option.

The New Moonraker

The Moonraker was now on a Kombi base with deluxe cab trim including brushed nylon seats and head restraints. A completely revised interior layout saw a complete kitchen and storage unit fixed along the offside of the vehicle. This included a stainless steel sink and drainer, electrically pumped water and a double burner cooker with grill and built-in splash guard. Beneath the sink was a large cool box (or optional fridge), and below the cooker were two drawers, one for cutlery, and a roomy double cupboard. To the right of the cooker was a large storage locker with hinged flap top with a vented gas bottle storage cupboard underneath. On the offside of the rear compartment was an upright storage cupboard with three cubby-hole shelves to the rear; a roof locker above the area was also still standard. The table was stored under this when not in use. The table was supported with a central chrome leg, which fitted into a template on the floor. This enabled the table to rotate for different uses, or even to make getting in and out easier!

Behind the passenger's seat was a wardrobe with access doors on both sides. A fold-down single rear-facing upright seat (or buddy seat) was fixed to the face of the wardrobe and an additional single seat could attach to this seat to make a double seat for dining. The rear bench seat pulled out to form the double bed. Buttoned foam cushioning was finished in a brown and beige check with brown vinyl on the reverse, and the curtains were in matching brown/beige check.

Despite being a Kombi base, the Moonraker was available in Pastel White, or Marino Yellow/Taiga Green/Mexico Beige under white.

Louvred windows provide excellent ventilation, especially when sited by the kitchen area.

The example shown here is a fully restored 1978 Moonraker currently owned by Lawrence Gibbons. The bodywork had been fully restored by a previous owner, but the interior just needed tidying. The spare wheel has been relocated to allow easy access to the engine.

The kitchenette features a fridge, stainless steel cooker and grill, and a sink unit with drainer. This arrangement proved both popular and practical.

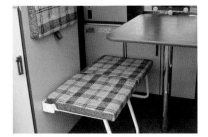

Units are arranged along the side opposite the sliding window. A wardrobe, with folding buddy seat, is sited by the sliding door.

The table is mounted on a single pedestal chrome leg.

Extra seating is via an extension to the buddy seat across the gangway.

The high position pull-out bed uses the rear deck area.

Paired bunk-beds are suspended beneath the elevating roof.

A linen cupboard and open storage areas are sited at the end of a deep storage cupboard, which adjoins the kitchen units. The table stores under the roof locker when not in use.

The Sundowner

The Sundowner was the first time Devon used a Panel Van as a standard base for a camping conversion, although the living area interior trim and furnishings were the same as for the Moonraker. Like its predecessors, the Sundowner doubled as a people carrier through its reversible double front bench seat. The bed unit was a pull-out affair, as for the Moonraker, but the wardrobe was sited in the rear where the spare wheel normally resided and the roof locker had no door.

Behind the sliding door at the end of the rear bench seat was a sink/drainer unit with electrically pumped water from a 5gal water container. A swing-out cooker was fitted to the left of the sliding door, which could be removed to create more floor space. The table was finished in chocolate and had extra legs for outside use.

Sundowners were all single colour finished in Pastel White, Marino Yellow, Taiga Green or Brilliant Orange.

1980–90: THE T25 CAMPERS

Devon saw no reason to start from scratch when the new generation T3 (T25) Transporters were introduced. Their Moonraker and Sundowner conversions in 1978 had been the result of twenty years of working with VW Buses. Years of experimenting with interior layouts and equipment had culminated in these two very successful and practical conversion layouts. So, in 1980, their new range, based on the new shape Transporter, carried the same names and the same basic layouts. All that was really different was the actual vehicle itself – a world away from the old air-cooled workhorse. One major departure, however, was that the new style Devon Double Top elevating roof, introduced as optional in 1978, became standard on both models.

The brochure for the new range showed European locations as well as UK ones, and took a very unusual approach by using the Recipe Style of text to describe the features and attractions of the new range.

A 1978 Sundowner with Double Top roof.

The T25 Moonraker

Finished in two tone – either Samos Beige over Aswan Brown or Ivory over Brilliant Orange, Agate Brown or Bamboo Yellow – the interiors were colour coded in complementary browns, beiges and oranges and reflected a new, more luxurious feel in keeping with the demands of a more prosperous leisure market. Cab seats were finished in brown brushed nylon and fitted with head restraints, buttoned deep foam cushions were finished in soft velour in open diamond check tones, Flotex carpet (hard wearing and stain resistant) was used on the floors and rich carpet style trim covered all interior panels – in dark brown up to window level and above in beige.

The Moonraker layout was essentially the same as its Bay Window predecessor, with the kitchen unit extending along the side behind the driver's seat. This unit had three main sections – a stainless steel sink and drainer with tap and push button electric pump under which was a fridge (optional) and double cupboard, the cooker with a drop-down flap, and the large storage chest unit at the end. If the optional fridge was not ordered then a portable cool box was supplied and stored here.

The wardrobe moved to the rear above the engine compartment at the end of the sink/cooker unit and behind this, just inside the tailgate, was a water carrier for filling the water tank. The water tank could be filled in situ, or removed and wheeled to a water supply. The single seat behind the passenger seat now became a proper seat with storage space under, and extended to become a two seater for dining and so on. The rear bench seat pulled out for the bed, and storage was accessed from the front of the bench. The table was still a centre leg table that could be rotated. The sink/cooker units were all finished in white or beige with wood effect or brown doors and trim, whilst the seat bases were finished in wood-look melamine-faced chipboard.

Optional extras included 12V/gas, RM 122 Electrolux fridge, Porta Potti chemical toilet, Kangol child safety seat, fire extinguisher, side step and a cab hammock bunk.

This 1980 Devon Moonraker is owned by Kev and Sue Edwards. Originally in brown and beige, the bottom half of the van has been sprayed to match the top, transforming the look of the vehicle. A Caravelle grille and headlight set, Mercedes wheels and a lowering job finish the look. Inside is fully original, apart from the Burberry upholstery, which complements the exterior perfectly.

The T25 Sundowner

The new Sundowner was also closely modelled on its Bay Window version and continued to be marketed by Devon as a multi-purpose vehicle, ideal for families. Based on the Kombi, the trim level was just standard in the cab; the above window areas in the living areas were not covered. The same basic upholstery and fabric colours were used as for the Moonraker (that is, variations on brown, orange and beige), but floor covering was patterned vinyl. The sliding front two-seater bench could be arranged for travel or dining with a simple swivelling backrest and the table folded up from the side for use with a single screw-in leg. The cooker was a two-burner portable unit, stored in a flap-down cupboard behind the passenger seat (much like the 1971 Devonette), and the gas bottle was stored behind the backrest of the single seat in a vented compartment. As well as the usual storage space there was a locker on the engine compartment deck. Two fresh water containers holding 5gal in all and a plastic washing-up bowl were stowed at the rear, but these and the wardrobe were sited on the passenger side, unlike the Moonraker. The pull-out bed was sited on the offside of the vehicle.

Options included a child's safety seat, fire extinguisher, side step and cab hammock bunk. The Sundowner was available in Pastel White, Orient Red or Brilliant Orange. Interior fabric finishes were the same patterns and colours as for the Moonraker.

1982: The Sunrise

By 1982 the Moonraker had become Devon's main VW conversion and the elevating roof changed design to the Aerospace Roof. This lifted straight up from a full length base, with the front part being higher than the rear, and it included a roof vent with flyscreen. The interior layouts and fitments were essentially the same, however.

A more luxurious version of the Moonraker was introduced, called the Sunrise. Identical in concept to the Moonraker, it offered a higher level of interior finish and fittings. The main changes included a matching vitreous enamel sink and gas hob to replace the stainless steel versions. The fridge was a large 2cu ft model with three-way power. The upholstery was best-quality Dralon, the curtains were thick, soft velvet and touch catches were fitted to all cabinet doors.

The interior cabinets were all finished in white with brown trim and worktops to match the exterior single colour of white with orange and yellow detail striping.

1986: The Eurovette and Caravette Models Return!

By 1986 Devon were busy converting Transits, Bedfords and Toyota models, but added two new models to their VW range, resurrecting the names Eurovette and Caravette to capitalize on the success of these models from previous times.

The new Eurovette was the flagship of the range and featured a stylish,

1986 Eurovette.

aerodynamic Hi-Top fixed roof. Aimed at a very different market from the family Camper it was designed to sleep two in comfort. The interior included cooker, oven, three-way fridge, hot box central heating, wardrobe, heated drying cabinet and fresh and waste water tanks with electric pump. Options included a water heater, microwave oven, Porta Potti and a beach shower unit with hot water for use outside at the rear of the vehicle.

The new Caravette featured a different style of elevating roof, with fully insulated rigid panels. This allowed for family use with a double or two single beds in the roof area, in addition to the main double bed. Like its 1970s predecessors this Caravette was designed to combine people carrier and Camper, with seating provided for seven, with all seats facing forwards, or with the first pair switched to face rearwards. Standard fittings included foldaway gas cooker, stainless steel pull-out sink unit with drainer and cutlery drawer, wardrobe and removable water tank with electric pump and two-way fridge. Options included a sunroof or the fixed Hi-Top (as on the Eurovette) in place of the elevating roof. Both Moonraker and Sunrise models continued to form part of the Devon range.

1989: UNDER NEW MANAGEMENT AND THE T4 CONVERSIONS

In 1989 Devon sold off the motor caravan side of the business, after deciding to concentrate on Minibuses and welfare vehicles. The new owners bought the Devon name and all the jigs and moulds; the workforce even received some training in the old Devon factory. The Moonraker and Eurovette models began to be produced by the new company, but just one year later the new T4 Transporter platform was introduced. Devon's designers were not as impressed with the conversion potential for the T4 as they had been with the T3 (T25) version and began to develop new models on the LWB Toyota. In 1992 the new company relocated to County

Durham with brand new facilities and in 1996 moved to their current location in Ferryhill, which is a large factory with room for further expansion. They currently produce a full range of conversions and are a Toyota-approved converter, with Toyota now forming the largest portion of their production.

The VW models produced on the T4 base were designated the Moonraker and the Aurora, and these 'new' Devons paid tribute to their heritage as being 'the culmination of Devon's long history of VW conversions'. Both versions featured a sloped aerodynamic fixed Hi-Top with side windows and were available in petrol, diesel, automatic or Syncro versions.

The Moonraker conversion was closely modelled on the traditional Moonraker layout, with the kitchen, fridge and wardrobe along the offside behind the driver and a rear bench seat.

The Aurora, however, was a totally different design, comprising a fully equipped kitchen with two single beds in the front. This allowed access through both rear and side doors and the forward-facing seats were sited directly behind the cab. Both cab seats swivelled to make a dinette in the front and a privacy curtain enabled the interior to be used as two separate sections.

Both models came fully equipped with stainless steel two-burner hob with grill and matching sink, a large 60cu ft fridge, mains hook-up, auxiliary battery and charger. Interior fittings for the Moonraker were finished in white, whilst the Aurora used oak veneer.

2004: THE T5

The Devon Moonraker V carries the traditional Moonraker layout into the new century, and reintroduced a rear-hinged low profile elevating roof. Within months of its launch it was awarded The Caravan Club Motor Caravan Design and Drive Competition 2004 Award for vans up to £28,500. The judges declared the Moonraker as a 'daily driver par excellence – a cracking Camper'.

Devon Conversions are based in Ferryhill, Co. Durham.
Telephone: 01740 655700
Website: www.devonconversions.com

The Martin Walter company was founded in 1773; originally harness manufacturers, they soon moved into building coaches and carriages. With the arrival of the motor car they began to produce bespoke coachwork on Rolls-Royce and Daimler bodies. In the early 1950s they identified a need for a vehicle that combined utility and family use from observing traders putting cushions into their vans at weekends for the family! The story goes that one of the Martin Walter directors noticed that people were sleeping in their vehicles whilst waiting for cross-channel ferries and came up with the idea of designing a vehicle that could be used to sleep in as well as travel in. In 1952, using a Bedford CA, they designed and produced a model that allowed seats to form a bench for sleeping and soon after that cookers were fitted. The name Dormobile (based on the French word dormir = to sleep) was coined by another company director and by 1956 the raising roof and swivel seats that folded in various ways had become Dormobile trademarks. Around this time the factory moved into new premises at the Tile Kiln Works at Folkestone and full-scale production of Dormobiles began. No other converter was as well set up and Dormobile soon became the main producer of affordable Campers, using mainly Bedfords, Landrovers, Austin J4s and Standard 10 vehicles.

The name Dormobile had already become established as a name associated with affordable yet quality motor caravans and the move into the VW market in 1960 reflected both the potential size of the market and the recognition of a very different style and image brought by the VW Bus. In fact, Dormobile has become one of those eponymous words like Biro and Hoover, whereby a brand name becomes its apparent generic name in the mind of the public. The quality and success of the famous Dormobile Martin Walter elevating roof was such that it was adopted by Devon as a standard option from 1962–67 instead of their own version, and Westfalia also offered the Dormobile roof as an

THE VOLKSWAGEN DORMOBILE 4-BERTH CARAVAN
PRICE £915 COMPLETE (U.K.) *(No Purchase Tax)* Dual Colours Extra

The 1962 Brochure cover shows off the Dormobile roof.

option for camping equipment SO 44 and early Bay Window models.

Dormobile ran into financial problems in the late 1970s and never converted any of the T25 models, concentrating on other marques. In 1984 the business ceased trading. However, in the late 1990s former employees resurrected the business and now supply genuine spare Dormobile parts such as roof canvases, skylights, name badges and so on.

1961: THE VW DORMOBILE IS LAUNCHED

In October 1961 the new 'Volkswagen – Dormobile' debuted at the Earl's Court Motor Show with the slogan, 'Famous the world over, Volkswagen and the Dormobile Caravan. Here is another fine Dormobile conversion – a real home on wheels with that sleek, smart Continental look.' It was available through the main VW Agents – VW Motors of St John's Wood, London, as Dormobile had successfully negotiated becoming an officially approved VW converter and so their conversions carried full VW warranty. (Only Devon carried similar backing at that time.)

Based on the VW Microbus bulkhead model, the most distinctive and obvious feature was the large side-hinged PVC elevating roof sited in the middle of the vehicle. This Martin Walter patent design had long been

fitted to other conversion platforms, but was one of the first roofs of its kind to be fitted as standard to a VW, and caught competitors by surprise. The roof featured two large windows and even had a flashing light on the dash to warn the driver against moving off when the roof was raised. Immediately the possibilities of the VW were expanded by doubling the sleeping room and allowing standing up when stationary!

The interior featured the patented 'Dormatic' seating. This system was both ingenious and simple, and allowed several different possible layouts. Two pairs of individual seats in the load area could be arranged to face forwards (allowing travelling for seven) or rearwards for dining and could also slide together to make bench seats for three, or, with an easy to use folding system, could fold flat to take four passengers each side. The front and back seats folded down to make two single beds or could be slid together to make a 6ft by 4ft (1.8m by 1.2m) double bed. Another unique feature was the way the seats could be folded flat against the body sides so that the entire load area floor was clear.

All seats were trimmed in two-tone Duracour; flooring was of lino in harmonizing colours. Curtains were secured with press studs.

The kitchen unit was fitted at the rear of the vehicle and comprised a built-in two-burner Calor Gas cooker/grill on the left with adjoining sink, and a draining board over a middle storage cupboard. This was the first of Dormobile's models to be fitted with a push/pull pump tap, as opposed to the gravity tap fitted on their other models. A two-piece hinged cover folded back to reveal the cooker and grill, and beneath this was a small storage cupboard, which also housed the gas tap. The lid of the sink was hinged over at a slight angle from the horizontal to serve as a draining board. Additional storage was in the under-sink cupboard and roof locker. To the right of the sink unit was a wardrobe. A folding dressing mirror was fixed with a catch on the side of the wardrobe to hold it in position. A folding step just ahead of the sink unit was positioned to assist in accessing the roof bunks.

A special carrier secured the gas bottle in the engine compartment and 7gal (32ltr) of water were stored in two fibreglass (later plastic) water tanks, the smaller of which was fitted with a handle and cap for easy carrying and filling.

A fluorescent light was fitted to the front of the roof aperture and an additional light was fitted over the cooker.

Unlike many other conversions, the cabinet work was initially all of steel, which must have caused some condensation problems! New plastic-covered furniture was introduced in late 1962 for the 1963 models.

Such was the appeal of this new VW Dormobile that just one year later *Autocar* reported:

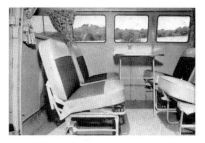

Initially cabinet work was in painted steel, which must have caused some condensation problems.

Several arrangements of sink/cooker/wardrobe were used during the sixties.

Last year's addition of the VW Microbus to the range of basic vans on which the Martin Walter Dormobile conversion is available is a pleasant surprise. The interior construction and layout are similar to those used in the Landrover Dormobile and, in the 12 months since its introduction, it has become one of the most popular motor caravans of this type on the market.

The literature of the time encapsulated the aspirational lifestyle of middle England: 'As well as being an ideal home on wheels, it is a mobile grandstand at races, sports meetings, gymkhanas and other outdoor displays of all kinds. If the weather is unkind, the huge roof windows give an excellent viewpoint, refreshments are laid on and the radio is an optional extra.' Changes in our use of language are especially interesting; the 1963 publicity literature read, next to a picture of two women relaxing in the hammock bunk beds: 'Right at the Top for Comfort! And not only for comfort but for gay good looks and sheer ingenuity of the time, this latest VW Dormobile is right at the top of the popularity poll!'

The VW Dormobile was founded on proven design and interior layouts and, as such, remained essentially the same throughout the Split Bus years, although from around 1965 the cooker was moved to the right. The main change was to colour matching of fabrics to new VW exterior colours.

Colour Combinations for 1962 are shown in the table overleaf.

Later body colours used the same basic colour harmonizing pattern. Grey or cream was the matching colour for the two-tone or piping for the seats.

From 1963 it was also possible to order a two-berth Dormobile, without the elevating roof.

The Dormobile could be fully outfitted by selecting from a comprehensive range of optional extras and accessories. These included a chrome VW badge, chrome-plated bumpers, a roof rack, loose seat covers, fire extinguisher, screenwashers (hand pump or 6V electric version), a car fan with rubber vanes, electric dash clock, 6V electric socket for a kettle, twin reversing lights, Ranger Foglamps or Roadlamps and Utilecon Radiomobile 6V radio with aerial.

The optional camping equipment available was very comprehensive and included air beds and cushions, a folding plastic bath on a frame, canvas bucket, camp bed, Easicool fridge, electric kettle, pressure cooker, Swan triple saucepan sets, 6gal (27ltr) sink waste bags, sleeping bags, crockery and cutlery in cased sets or as individual items and a rubber torch. Also available was the Dormobile Tent awning with or without side panels, and a toilet tent. Of all the converters at the time, Dormobile offered by far the most comprehensive one-stop camping shop to outfit the vehicle.

The Dormobile shown here is a 1964 model, owned by Brian Ford. It has been fully restored and the seating re-covered using red leather instead of red vinyl. At the time of the photographs the wardrobe and kitchenette had not been refurbished and so were not fitted.

Body Colour	Upholstery	Roof Canvas
Dove Blue	Blue	Red/white stripe
Pale Grey	Red	Red/white stripe
Pearl White	Blue	Green/white stripe
Turquoise Green	Blue	Green/white stripe
Ruby Red	Red	Red/white stripe
Pearl White/Mouse Grey	Red	Red/white stripe
Blue White/Turquoise Green	Blue	Green/white stripe
Beige Grey/Sealing Wax Red	Red	Red/white stripe

A 1964 Dormobile.

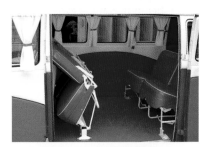

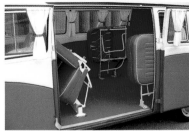

The Dormobile script badge is affixed to the cab door.

The patent Dormatic seating allowed a variety of layouts as well as all forward-facing or dinette style. For load carrying the seats folded and clipped against the front bulkhead and/or side walls. They laid flat to form two single beds, a double bed or day settee and seats.

Dormobile Volkswagen

The front cover of the 1969 brochure.

1968: THE BAY WINDOW DORMOBILES

The Dormobile Motor Caravan D4/6

The new shape gave Dormobile a chance to rethink both layout and design and, true to form, they came up with another innovative patent Dormobile design – the front seat fold-out cooker! In order to allow more height in the cab area for cooking the elevating roof was moved forwards by about a foot.

Based on the Kombi, and thus usually finished in a single colour, the interior was remodelled to create more living space. All units were finished in wood-grained light grey or cream melamine, with a moulded sink and drainer supplied by water pumped from two 3.5gal (16ltr) water tanks. The sink unit ran down the offside sidewall behind the driver's seat and included a large 2cu ft cool box accessed from the top. Ample storage in this unit was in three cupboards, one of which held the water carriers. A long shelf with a lip edge was fitted above the sink unit. A wardrobe was affixed to the bulkhead behind the passenger seat, against which a fold-down single seat was sited. Seating was arranged round a table with a fold-down leg; this attached to the long cabinet side and was stored beneath the rear bench seat when not in use. The bench seat ran across the rear and was raised to form the high double bed along one side. Upholstery was in wool moquette and

finished in gold or poppy red with contrasting PVC borders. There was also a large bedding locker above the engine bay behind the rear seat.

The most innovative feature, which released valuable space in the living area, was the cooker, housed in a rehinged front seat. The cooker shield was stowed behind the front passenger seat when not in use and the whole front cab seat tipped forwards to access the fold-up cooker and grill unit. As with the previous versions, a warning light on the dash was fitted, which flashed when the ignition was switched on and the roof was still elevated. The roof canvas was either red and white or green and white. A two-berth version with a fixed roof was also available. Optional extras included underseal, a child's cab bunk, chrome hubcaps, tent awnings and a roof rack as well as the full range of Dormobile camping essentials and accessories.

Interestingly, it was also possible to order an LHD conversion. Dormobiles

were known and exported all round the world, and even manufactured under licence in some countries such as Australia.

The Camper shown here is a 1972 model owned by Glenn and Jill Taylor, and known affectionately as 'Ollie'. It has had three previous owners, the first owner covering only 28,000 miles (45,050km) in twenty-two years of ownership, which helps to account for its excellent condition. It has never been welded and has no body filler, although it has been touched up here and there and the front panel has been sprayed over. Since acquiring the Bus, Glenn has fitted electronic ignition, an oil temp dipstick and a bugpack. Other practical enhancements are an electric water pump, leisure battery and an Eberspächer heater – hence the control box which can be seen on the rear bulkhead. Glenn says they deliberately sought out a Dormobile as they liked the 'all down one side' layout and the roof style.

This 1972 D4/6 is in original, pristine condition (although the seats have been re-covered very tastefully). For the Bay models the elevating roof was moved forwards and the cabinets ran down one side.

The worktop on the cabinet lifts up to reveal the sink with an electric pump tap. The water container is sited in the cabinet underneath.

At the end of the cabinet run is a cool box and additional storage.

Dining mode.

Light wood-grain veneer for the table top and cabinets give a bright, modern look.

The original fabric can be seen on this Camper; one of the first things to wear and be replaced.

The table and rear deck are used to form a high position bed.

The (removable) wardrobe is mounted on the front bulkhead.

Water is stored under the sink. Attached to the door is a canvas waste bin in the same fabric as the elevating roof.

The front passenger seat tips forward …

… for access to the cooker which is stored neatly behind.

1970: THE DORMOBILE D4/8

In 1970 Dormobile introduced a totally new version of the VW to their range, designed to hit the multi-purpose vehicle market, but the luxury rather than the economy end. Based on either Kombi (single colour) or Microbus (two-tone paint) models, it was designed to seat eight people in the forward-facing position and also sleep four adults (plus child in optional cab bunk). Versatility of use was the keynote in its design.

For the first time a refrigerator was available (also for the D4/6) and a fitted, removable, gold-coloured carpet was added for a touch of luxury. Curtains were soft orange with matching seat upholstery in gold woven Evlan material. The Kombi model side panels were trimmed in fawn PVC, whilst the Microbus retained the original VW trim.

The cooker folds out and has a metal extension side shelf that clips onto the front seat. The controls face the driver's seat.

A folding buddy seat attaches to the front of the wardrobe.

The fully upholstered seating used steel-framed panelled box storage units and made up into a low-level double bed or single bed with outer seats at the bed sides. For travelling, the seats faced forwards and for dining they were arranged around the

Another folding seat can be positioned in the gangway …

… to create seating for four around the table.

The 1972 D4/8; designed as people carrier and weekend Camper. The upholstery shown is not original but the curtains and gold carpets are.

For travelling all seats can face forwards. Note the matching footmats across the seat runners.

Dining mode. The seat backs lift and reposition in the seat base. The foot mats store behind the front seats by the bulkhead.

melamine table, which fixed to the right side wall. This table doubled as a facia for the cooker and wash unit at the rear of the vehicle.

At the rear above the engine compartment next to the spare wheel was a unit which housed two 3.5gal water containers and a storage locker with plastic, removable washbasin. Next to this was a double-burner cooker, which could be used in situ, or removed and made self-supporting on its own legs to stand outside. On the offside was a wardrobe with a horizontal sliding shutter. Also fitted was an eye-level vanity mirror.

The D4/8 was available with or without the Dormobile elevating roof and other options were as for the D4/6 Caravan version.

The 1972 D4/8 shown here has just been acquired by Simon Edgington and had been owned from new by the previous owner. Because it is quite a basic Camper the model was not as popular as the D4/6, and very few have survived with all the original fittings. Simon plans to restore it and refurbish the interior, and has already made a start by re-covering the seats.

Ready for lunch!

Seats slide into different positions on metal runners and lock into place.

Rear deck arrangement. The cooker can be used from inside, or lifted out and mounted on legs. The wardrobe, sited on the left, is also removable. A simple wood unit on the right houses the water containers and a wash bowl.

Rear view showing the straps for securing the gas bottle (carried in the engine compartment when not in use) and storage areas in the water cabinet.

Seat backs lift out and lay between base units to form the double (or single) beds.

The cab bunk drops onto two bars that are positioned across the door openings.

eurec

Nieuw in Holland:
eurec
Volkswagen Campers

CASSANDRA

PANDORA

De Eurec Cassandra camper.

Van dak tot vloer op luxe ingesteld.

In 1978 the Ben Pon dealership in Holland offered Europe a new style of Camper, quite different from the Westfalia models. Called the Eurec, it featured, as standard, a full length, side-hinged elevating roof and was available in two models – the Cassandra and the Pandora. The Cassandra featured fridge, cooker, sink and storage along one side, with a fold-down buddy seat by the sliding door. The Pandora had a sink at the end of the bench seat and a swing-out cooker mounted on the bulkhead.

In fact, these conversions were actually Devon models – with the Cassandra being the new Moonraker layout and the Pandora the Devon Eurovette! The roof was the newly introduced Devon Double Top option.

The only difference was that the interior layouts were configured for LHD and Devon badging was omitted. It is unclear if Devon supplied the Pon dealership with interiors to fit, or if Pon supplied Devon with LHD base units for conversion; however, with import/export duties it is likely that Devon supplied Pon with all the fitments. Interestingly, the first brochure actually used Devon RHD brochure pictures and was printed in Bristol, though layout drawings showed LHD configuration!

The relationship between Pon and Devon continued into the T25 range, with the new style Devon Moonraker layout still marketed in LHD form as the Cassandra, available from December 1979.

The 1964 brochure shows the earlier style load door cabinet.

The 1965 brochure cover is reminiscent of a gameshow hostess showing the prizes on offer!

EZ (pronounced E–Zee as in Easy!) Campers were another US company which recognized that the growing demand for Westfalia Campers far exceeded supply. Based in Littlerock, California, the company began converting Panel Vans around 1963/4. As well as supplying conversions, they also proudly declared 'EZ Camper will convert your VW 211 van into a wonderful weekend cabin on wheels!' This accounts for the variations found on EZ conversions.

The model was called El Viajero (the Traveller) and, like Sundial, Riviera and other US conversions, it was closely modelled on the Westfalia interior. Blazoned across brochures, the words 'Beautiful! Practical! Versatile! Compact!' encapsulated everything the company stood for. Although at first glance very similar to the Sundial, the interior specification was more luxurious.

The 1965 EZ Camper opposite was based on a Kombi, meaning EZ did not have to fit crank windows, and features an original factory option of six pop-out side windows. Unusually, plain birch panels were fitted instead of the EZ grooved wood panel style. The fitments are all original, including the striped, fringed awning. The Bus was donated by Dane Dawson to the Arizona Bus Club, who refurbished and repainted it to use as a charity fund-raising raffle prize at their annual

Photographs from the brochure show the EZ in use. The awning had detachable sides for complete privacy.

event, the Jerome Jamboree, in 2004. At this stage the Bus still needed new paint and a rear bumper.

The EZ interior was fully insulated with diamonized polyclad plywall, with a distinctive grooved wood panelling effect, and the seating was vinyl covered. The rear bench seat had automatically activated legs and converted in seconds into a 6ft 2in (1.9m) bed. A Westfalia style wardrobe, with mirror mounted on the door, was sited by the rear loading door with roof locker and rear storage cupboard. The rear load door unit was initially an open slatted cupboard, but from 1965 this was a shelved cupboard with an oval door, matching the wardrobe style door.

Behind the front seat by the load door was a 50lb cool box/12gal (55ltr) water tank with pump unit, with a fold-down flap on the side for a plastic washing bowl. The front load door had a folding shelf table on which to stand the two-burner Coleman cooker. Five side windows were fitted, made of safety glass with aluminium frames and screens. An extra wall light was fitted above the table and two folding tables were supplied, with Nevamor tops and chrome trim. Chrome trim was also fitted round cabinet door and folding shelf edges. A child's cab bunk was standard with an optional sleeping mat for another child to sleep across the bench seat.

Mounts were fitted to the roof and front bumper for the fringed, striped awning that had removable side walls and a private area for a chemical toilet.

From 1966 a version based on the Kombi, with optional two-tone paint,

The finished restoration ready to be raffled off! The Westfalia influences in the interior design and layout are clear to see. All the work needed to bring the Bus into this condition was carried out by ABC members; what a prize that was for the lucky winner!

was also available. This featured the new style of bed support using an aircraft design pre-stressed substructure, instead of fold-down legs, and a fully sprung seat base. New style gearcranked opening side windows were available as an option. Also optional was the roof rack, which came in two different sizes. Like Sundial and Riviera, EZ also offered as options both the official VWoA side mirrors, commonly known as 'elephant ear'

mirrors and 'truck' mirrors for better rear vision.

This unusual EZ model (below), featuring loading doors on both sides and Westfalia cabinets, is owned by Paul and Francis Bond, who saw it whilst on holiday in Florida and promptly fell in love with it! It had been driven all the way across the US from California in the late sixties and, on arrival in Florida, the owner promptly sold it to raise cash. The

VWoA offered two alternative side mirrors.

A 1967 double door EZ conversion with two-tone paint and Westfalia rack and ladder.

Top-hinged crank opening windows like this were off the shelf RV parts; similar versions can be found on other US Campers such as the Sundial.

Three windows were fitted down one side, two in the other side to allow for the wardrobe. One window in each side is fitted with a mesh flyscreen.

Interior 'wood panelling' effect is a distinctive feature of EZ conversions.

The Westfalia cool box/sink unit is the same as found on 1968 Campmobiles, suggesting the van was converted around that time.

The bench seat is a pull-out bed. Note the wood ply headlining and Westy roof shelf.

The sink lid flaps over to form a useful table/worktop.

The picnic and flask holder set clips over a seat and is a very cool American period accessory.

Load doors on both sides are not a common option, especially on a Camper, but make for excellent access to living and washing areas. The upper cooling vents are the tell-tale signs of a conversion based on a Panel Van.

buyer still had pictures of the Bus doing this trip, which showed the whitewall tyres and two-tone paint which existed at that time.

Two-tone paint with matching painted window frames was an option for EZ Campers, though their conversions on new vehicles normally used the Kombi as a base for this. Unusually, this Camper is a double door Panel Van, which actually makes access much easier. The EZ interior arrangement ideally lends itself to doors on both sides, allowing access for cooking/washing on one side and seating on the other. Access to the vehicle is made easier with the addition of a side step and Empi cab step. Another fascinating period accessory is the rubber drinks holder, which actually works, allowing the driver to keep cool with a Coke whilst driving! The period picnic set, which clips over a seat back and has twin flasks and a cool store section was a popular sixties accessory in the US.

The Bus features the EZ trademarks of crank-opening windows (two of which are aluminium screened) and grooved wood panelling for that 'cabin in the woods' feel. Whilst the vinyl seat covers appear to have been replaced with two-tone vinyl at some point, they retain the original look. The wardrobe, wash cabinet and roof shelf all carry Westy 'Campmobile' stickers and are probably Westfalia originals fitted by EZ, who, like other US converters, sometimes actually bought in and used Westfalia furniture! The wash cabinet also has the Westy style lid, which flaps into the middle to form an extra table. Some typical EZ features, like the loading door spice rack cabinet and the door-mounted cooker shelf, are not present – possibly these were removed, but it is more likely that this van was taken to EZ for private conversion to a customer's requirements. The fact that it is a double door conversion and there is no EZ badge supports this possibility. The Campmobile cabinet styles on this conversion were used by Westfalia from 1968, so it would seem likely that the Bus was converted by EZ around that time, rather than from new.

Richard Holdsworth Conversions, based in Ashford, Middlesex, started converting new and used Campers on the VW Bay Window model (and the Commer) in 1967. Soon after, they began to offer kit versions of the conversion and, by 1972 as the name became established, they had moved to larger premises near Reading. The new factory was sited in a disused WWII aerodrome and boasted fifteen assembly bays where up to fifty Campers could be assembled at any one time, and production doubled from 150 to 300 units per day! VW models formed just a small part of the conversion range, but the name Holdsworth soon became recognized as a major player in the motor caravan trade. As well as hand-built quality wood furniture, Holdsworth also used exclusive Scandinavian weave fabrics and would convert a used van as well as offering a full range of DIY conversion kits, units and parts. Comparatively few Bay Window models survive intact, but the T25 (Villa and Vision) and T4 (Valentine) generations of Holdsworth conversions set new standards in luxury and appointment, and many are still in original condition and in use today. In 1995 the company went into receivership and, although soon relaunched as Cockburn Holdsworth, never really recovered. Richard and his wife Heather were kept on as design consultants and Richard went on to work with Auto-Sleeper to develop their range of conversions.

THE BAY WINDOW HOLDSWORTHS

There were two main interior layouts; Layout 1 was the basic model with the kitchen unit sited by the sliding door at the end of a bench seat. This consisted of a cool box with a demountable cooker on top for cooking inside or out. To the rear of this was a pump tap for a washing bowl, with foot-operated electric pump. Seating was arranged dinette style round the table, which laid between the bench seats for the bed. Layout 2 had a stainless steel sink and drainer mounted in the kitchen cabinet, above the cool

A 1974 press advert showing Layout 1 with dark veneer cabinets.

'Active' camping scenes were typical of the time; this 1976 advert shows the Layout 1 elevating roof model with the cooker/cool box at the side of the rear bench.

Layout 2 had a sink/cool box cabinet sited at the side of the rear bench and the cooker behind the front passenger.

The full length, side-hinged, elevating roof was a Holdsworth design.

box, a high level bed using the table and space above the engine, and a unit behind the front passenger by the sliding door, on top of which the demountable cooker was sited. It also had a corner fold-out single seat.

Furniture was in solid wood Scandinavian timber, which received four coats of varnish and upholstery was in modern, hard-wearing, bright Scandinavian weave fabric. A roof cupboard was standard. A side step and louvred side window opposite the sliding door were optional, and a patent Richard Holdsworth front-mounted spare wheel carrier was also available. By the early 1970s there were two elevating roof options: a

Camping in style.

New harmonizing fabrics complement original cabinets and worksurfaces.

The rear wardrobe has a bottom hinged door and additional interior light above to the side.

Twin bunks were fitted in the pop-top roof.

The high position bed uses the rear deck area. Note the fluorescent light by the sink unit.

The cooker in Layout 2 was sited behind the passenger against the bulkhead.

The electric footpump switch for the tap can be seen on the floor at the end of the rear bench.

The original maker's nameplates are often missing and almost impossible to replace.

side-hinged full length elevating roof with gold/yellow/brown striped canvas and a concertina style pop top called the Weathershield. The latter was a low profile, one-piece, shaped aluminium roof, which was designed for Holdsworth by the same people who fabricated the alloys for Concorde.

Many people had roofs or kits fitted to their Buses, as in the example on page 6 which was originally a Devon, but some time in the late 1970s had a Holdsworth roof and some of the interior units fitted from the DIY range.

Advertising by Holdsworth in the late 1970s concentrated on debunking claims from rival conversions to emphasize the build quality of the Holdsworth, as in this blurb from 1977:

> Some motor caravans steal your heart when you read the colourful adverts. Adjectives flow when they describe their advanced elevating roofs and giant sized water tanks. But out on the road things don't always work out so well. The roofs sit so high on the van the drag causes your VW to drink fuel … with such a bulky roof you'd think the roof bunks would be of generous adult size but in reality they are not. And the giant water tank can't be cleaned out.
>
> Not so with a Richard Holdsworth. The roof is the tried and tested Weathershield, much easier to raise or lower and with a low profile that gets on well with everyone, car parks, ferries and your pocket. Our water tanks can get cleaned out whenever you want and they are not under-slung to get knocked off at first sight of a lumpy caravan pitch. We've got a sensible high level bed that gives you floor space 24 hours a day … plus lots of genuine timber with not a single trace of cheap and nasty chipboard.

Holdsworth conversions won many awards for their design and build quality and this tradition continued with the advent of the new T25.

The Camper featured here is a 1972 Holdsworth, with pop-top roof, owned by Kavan and Joanna O'Connell. The Layout 2 features can clearly be seen in the photographs. The upholstery has been tastefully updated to complement the light cabinet work and exterior paint work (Chianti Red).

THE T25 HOLDSWORTHS

By the mid-eighties the VW T25 conversions carried out by Richard Holdsworth were setting a standard for others to follow, and the conversion was awarded Motor Caravan of the Year in 1987/88 and again in 1988/89. The quality of the finish and furnishing was such that *Motor Caravan* magazine summed it up as, 'a definite air of quality and standard of finish that put it amongst the very best.'

Light ash furniture with hand-finished beech edgings, coupled with specially selected classy fabrics, gave a

sense of luxury and airy spaciousness. The VW range consisted of two models with very different layouts – the Villa and the Vision.

THE HOLDSWORTH VILLA 3

In 1985 the Villa 2 had been voted Best Elevating Roof Motor Caravan at the Motor Show and The Villa 3, launched in 1987 showed even more improvements. The sink and hob unit ran along the wall opposite the sliding door, with a three way Electrolux fridge beneath the hob unit. The cooker, sink and drainer were a one piece section, finished in vitreous enamel. The gas

cylinder, stored in the base, slid out on a tray at the touch of a finger meaning changing the cylinder was considerably easier! Continuing along the side towards the rear from the sink/cooker unit was more storage including a cocktail cabinet. The Zig unit for the leisure battery and mains hook-up was mounted above this. The rear bench unit was a rock-and-roll style pull-out bed, with a section for the chemical toilet under the end nearest the sliding door. The rotating multi position table could be centrally mounted or fixed between the single seat and front passenger swivel seat.

The conversion was available with fixed roof, Holdsworth elevating roof or with VW factory high top roof (Villa HT). This HT model gave permanent standing room and had extra storage at the front above the cab, and at the rear, as well as an optional lift out shelf.

THE HOLDSWORTH VISION

The Vision was based on the VW High Roof model and featured a very different arrangement, more like an RV or motorhome, with rear-end kitchen, separate toilet compartment and L-shaped dinette making the interior feel as if there were two separate rooms! A folding door divided the rear section off for privacy when washing or using the toilet, which was stored under the rear seat and accessed from the kitchen end. This area measured 4ft by 2ft (1.2m by 0.6m) – bigger than that in some American motorhomes of the time! The woodworking and interior finish and fitments were of the same high standard that characterized all Holdsworth conversions. The layout allowed for four forward-facing seats, an L-shaped dinette and, by reclining the driver seat and swivelling the front passenger seat, a very spacious and comfortable living area could be created. An optional roof bed made the vehicle able to sleep four adults in comfort. The swivel table also allowed a variety of seating/dining arrangements. The unique layout, spacious interior, and quality fitments made the Vision one of the best equipped and luxurious VW Campers of the time, and set new standards that would soon become the norm when the T4 generation arrived.

The Vision featured an L-shaped seating/dining layout …

1989 range profiling the Villa 3 and the Vision. The Villa set new standards for motorhomes and won many awards.

… with a fully fitted kitchen area at the rear.

The Villa 3 interior featured a luxurious, well-appointed layout.

The Villa 3 was the elevating roof version.

The Vision was the fixed high roof model.

Joch Camping Einrichtung was a Hannover based Karosserie that began converting VWs into Campers around 1956.

The interior layout was similar to the Westfalia SO 34 in that the seating was L-shaped, with a bench running under the side windows to meet a rear bench seat, making seating for five. A wardrobe was sited at the end of the rear bench by the load door. The rectangular table attached to the front bulkhead and a small unit by the front load door contained a cooker and crockery cupboard. The table could be used outside by mounting it at the end of this unit. Westfalia style check fabric and wooden headlining finished the inside, and a small pop-up roof vent/skylight was fitted. One interesting feature was the fitting of twelve small pocket pouches to the front load door for handy storage of a variety of things!

The Bay Window model featured the same layout and materials, except that the table was now mounted centrally because of the walk-through design. As well as converting new Campers, customers could also take their vehicles to Joch Camping to be kitted out, or buy pieces in kit form.

Die beste JOCH-Camping-Einrichtung, die es je gab

Bestechende Vorteile:
- Tagsüber vier bequeme Sitze am großen Tisch
- am Tage ein Bett und eine Kinderliege bereit
- nachts ein bequemes, breites Doppelbett und
- zwei Kinderliegen
- Kofferraum + Stauraum + viel Schränke
- bequeme Poister in „pflegeleicht"-Stoffen
- Seiten- und Rückfenster bleiben sichtfrei
- Fahrerdurchgang bleibt frei
- Einrichtung läßt sich leicht herausnehmen
- für alle VW-Modelle lieferbar

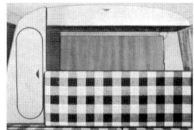

Kamper Kits of Monta Vista, California, were among the first US producers of camping kits for the VW Bus, producing a camping conversion, based on the Panel Van, from early 1962. Mounted on the rear load door was an open-fronted spice cabinet and a flap-down shelf on the front load door was used to stand the Coleman stove. Inside consisted of an icebox unit, with water storage and pump tap, a middle jump seat and single seat behind the driver. The icebox unit had a flap-down shelf for a washing bowl. Seating was arranged dinette style, with the rear seat come pull-out bed facing round a flap-down table fixed to the side wall. A Westfalia style wardrobe with door mirror was sited at the end of the bench seat by the load door. Louvred windows with safety glass and removable screens were standard, and a distinctive feature was a long picture window, with two sliding sections, opposite the load doors. The side walls and roof were insulated and panelled in ash, with seat upholstery in US naugahyde. Upholstery colours were chosen by the customer, with matching curtains.

A striped, fringed awning, with side walls and draughtproof skirt under the load doors, was part of the standard equipment.

The Karmann Mobil differed from the Jurgens (*see* Chapter 29) in that it did not have a Luton top over the front cab. The Karmann Karosserie had long had links with VW, with the Karmann Ghia and the Beetle Cabriolet probably being the most widely known VW conversions. In 1973–74 one of the family directors of the Karmann Karosserie, Wilhelm Karmann, visited South Africa and there came across a very different kind of VW based motor caravan – the Jurgens Auto Villa. There was nothing quite like it in Europe (apart from a few very expensive luxury Winnebago style conversions), and nothing like it on a VW base. He was so impressed with the vehicle that he successfully negotiated with Jurgens for the rights to build a version under licence.

In 1974 the Karmann Mobil was launched. It was very similar to the Jurgens model, with insulated aluminium cladding round an aluminium frame, but did not have the Luton top for extra sleeping space over the front cab. The walk-through cab led into a private bathroom area equipped with shower, sink and portable toilet, opposite which was an electric fridge and storage cupboards, stainless steel sink and two-burner hob. At the rear of the vehicle was the living area, raised from the rest of the floor area (to

create storage accessed at the rear of the vehicle), which was arranged in the traditional caravan style of U-shaped seating, all with windows, round a table. The table laid down to form a double bed.

THE KARMANN GIPSY

With the arrival of the T25 platform in 1979, Karmann updated the interior to the new dimensions, but basically kept the same, proven interior layout. Interestingly, they decided to use the original Jurgens feature of the Luton top over the cab to provide additional sleeping space, a feature which was

later to become common on RVs and coach-built Campers. The new model was designated the Karmann Gipsy.

The Karmann Gipsy pictured overleaf is owned by Alan Malone who purchased it in 2003 with just 63,000 miles (101,370km) on the clock. It was first registered in 1988 and is a right-hand drive, 1900cc petrol engine water-cooled type (wasserboxer). The original sales price in 1988 of around £22,000 put it right at the top end of the motor caravan range, but the price tag reflected the high spec of the fitments and finishing. It is fully insulated and designed for use all year round. The Karmann Gipsy was not built just for weekend use or shopping trips! Interior facilities include a 90ltr three-way fridge, two-ring gas hob with ceramic sink, twin batteries, a Truma system for gas-blown air central heating, a 10ltr (2.2gal) hot water cylinder for the shower or on tap for the bathroom and kitchen sinks, an inboard fresh water tank and a waste water tank underneath. All the windows, except the cab, are double glazed with integral fly/silver screen blinds. The bathroom area has a toilet, shower and hand basin, with a built-in wall cupboard with mirrored doors and a shower curtain.

In the main area there is a wardrobe and other storage for food, including a cutlery drawer and a bar! In the rear section is the living/dining/sleeping area with seats arranged U shape round a table. The table folds

The new style Karmann, with extension over the front cab, in a wilderness setting.

A 1988 Karmann Gipsy.

down to make the large bed, which is approx 6ft 5in x 4ft 6in. The double sleeping area over the cab is accessed by a ladder. There is an outside gas cylinder cupboard and outside locker storage under the back seat area.

The cheaper priced Karmann Cheetah was essentially the same vehicle, with fewer extras such as the chemical toilet.

The Karmann conversion represented a luxury camping lifestyle, but being based on a VW with 4WD options, meant it could cope with rugged terrain. The interior design remained essentially the same for the T4 range, as can be seen in the photographs below.

The kitchen area is on the same side as the door, behind the passenger.

The bathroom area is opposite the kitchen area, behind the driver.

The T4 range of Karmann Campers.

The coloured ceramic hob and sink unit are set into a modern worktop.

The seating rearranges to form a luxurious double bed.

The seating is arranged caravan style in the rear.

The new generation of Karmann Campers, based on the T5 platform, look stylish and sport a sleek, modern design.

The original advert launching the new range in 1958.

1958–59: THE AUTOHOME IS INTRODUCED

Leeds-based Moortown Motors was another UK firm to start converting VW Buses into Campers in the late 1950s, and the first demonstration models were shown at the 1958 Motor Show, a year after Devon. The conversion was initially based on the 1958 Microbus and the interior finish was matched to the 1958 two-tone dark over light green colour scheme of Palm Green over Sand Green with soft green upholstery.

Like Devon, Moortown co-operated with established local cabinet makers, in this case Bamforth of East Heslerton, who finished the wood-

work to a very high standard of craftsmanship. The cloth headliner was replaced with a PVC one flush to the roof and a translucent plastic roof ventilator was fitted as optional equipment. Child's berths used the front bench seat and the space over the engine compartment and the typical 'bench seats round a table' dinette formed the basis of the interior. Sited next to these were a sink with pumped water supply and upright crockery cupboard (fitted with crockery) at the rear, and a two-burner gas cooker with gas cylinder and Osokool cooling box underneath at the front. Under the cooker shelf was a cutlery drawer and storage cupboard; the cooker could be accessed by flap-down sides that allowed it to be used inside or outside the van. The large table top could be stowed under a roof cupboard when not in use and the bed was made up by laying a panel, stored behind the driver's seat, between the bench seats. Dunlopillo foam of 4in (100mm) thickness was used for the seat/bed cushions. A gas light was mounted above the windows facing the loading doors.

Japanese light oak was used throughout and the flooring was light green lino to match the upholstery and seat coverings. The table, sink and cooker lids were faced with green Formica. This colour scheme continued into 1959, with the new style two-tone paint now being light (Seagull Grey) over dark (Mango Green).

This beautiful example of a Moortown, owned by Jason Mallinson, has a totally original interior and is only missing the Osokool cool box under the cooker and the flexible water tank that originally sat under the sink unit and was shaped to fit the wheel arch. The interior is immaculate, although there have been repairs and new paint to some body areas.

Designated a Moortown Mark 1, it was bought in 1960 by a Dr Bellamy who only covered 50,000 miles (80,450km) in the next twenty-eight years. In 1988 it was bought with a seized engine and advertised in Volksworld for £4,000, which was very expensive at the time, probably reflecting both the rarity value and the original interior condition. Jason's father-in-law bought it for £3,000 and

The maker's enamel badge was fitted to the dash.

The large capacity enamelled washing bowl puts other sinks to shame!

The cab seat is still in immaculate condition. Note how the panelling complements the interior colour scheme.

For tall sleepers extra length was obtained by removing a panel on the front bench seat.

The Dudley two-burner cooker has hardly seen any use.

The crockery cupboard, with green interior finish, originally came fully equipped in the top of the range models.

The gas bottle was stored in the cooker unit and accessed by the door on the side. The Osokool cool box is missing and an authentic replacement still needs to be sourced.

set about some restoration. At some time, the rear lights had already been updated, a post-1963 rear corner had been fitted and one rear side panel had been replaced with a post-1963 panel featuring ten inward-facing cooling vents (instead of the pre-1963 nine outward-facing ones). Accident damage necessitated this perhaps? It was originally finished in Seagull Grey over Mango Green but he wanted a more distinctive look and so opted for a three-tone paint effect with the roof and lower body in Mango Green and the centre section in Velvet Green (interestingly, a 1958 Moortown advert shows this three-tone style of paint on their demonstration vehicle, a style which had also been used on some early Westfalia Campers). He also fitted a 1500cc single port engine, but then lost interest!

In 1992 Jason persuaded him to pass it on and since then has carried out some more updates. In 1994 he repainted the roof and subsequently had the Bus converted to 12V, lowered it and fitted IRS. He also painted all the 'hidden' parts of the interior in green hammerite and changed the original burnt orange curtains for softer, velvet ones in matching green. The documentation and handbooks are still housed in the original Moortown plastic wallet and even include an invoice from a woodyard to the cabinet makers, Bamforths, for wood used in the conversion!

Green Formica table and work surface tops and handbuilt oak furniture make the Moortown interior very distinctive. Flooring was also in green. The sink unit is on the right with a mirror above, mounted on the crockery cupboard door. The gas light with glass shade has been moved to here from the side wall and converted to run off the battery.

Luxurious PVC headliner and wood trim were typical Moortown features. A translucent, pop-up skylight was an innovative option back in 1958!

1960-62:
THE AUTOHOME MARK 1A AND 2A

For 1960 Moortown launched an extended range under the umbrella name Moortown Autohome, which included Standard and Atlas vans as well as two VW versions, now on the Kombi or Microbus and designated the Mark 1A and Mark 2A. Either version could be based on the Deluxe Microbus by special order. The Mark 1A was essentially the same as the previous VW Autohome, except that the gas lighting was dropped and updated with an extra fluorescent light, and the front cab seat base swung up to make child's bunk beds in the front. An additional cupboard on the rear loading door now housed a plastic washing-up bowl that swung down for use in position under the push/pull pump tap in the crockery unit. Two 6gal (27ltr) water carriers were housed under the pump. There was also a wardrobe, with a distinctively shaped door hinged to open out

at the end of the rear bench seat where the sink was formerly sited, and a pair of shelved cupboards in the rear area. The Mark 2A was essentially the same, but offered a higher level of trim and finish. A strap-over tent extension was also available as an optional extra.

1962: THE MARK 1B AND MARK 5 – ONE OF THE FIRST WALK-THROUGH LAYOUTS

In October 1962 Moortown revised their layouts and models, and now offered their 1963 Autohome range in two versions, designated the Mark 1B and the Mark 5. The new Mark 1B was essentially very similar to the previous versions, but the new innovation, ahead of its competitors, was the Mark 5, which was one of the first interiors to use a walk-through cab layout with divided front seats. The Mark 1B bench seats were moved further apart to create more space. The main table was slightly narrowed to make for better access and a supplementary table for

outside use doubled as the bed base when laid between the bench seats. A new style of cooker now featured a grill. The walk-through Mark 5 version had a rearranged dinette with a pull-out extension from the forward seat to fill the gap when the main bed was made up. This also doubled as a forward-facing seat complete with cushion for day use.

Because of the divided front seat the spare wheel had to be carried in the rear, over the engine compartment, and one of the water carriers had to be resited there too. This meant the loss of a child's berth, so a transverse stretcher was provided instead. The double bunk in the cab area was discontinued and returned to being a single berth on the bench seat. The cooker cabinet was also different in size and was mounted behind the passenger seat; other than that, both models were equipped identically. Later in 1963 the Mark 5 cooker unit was revised to become a cupboard similar to that of the 1B, with a

The new 1962 Moortown models introduced a walk-through option.

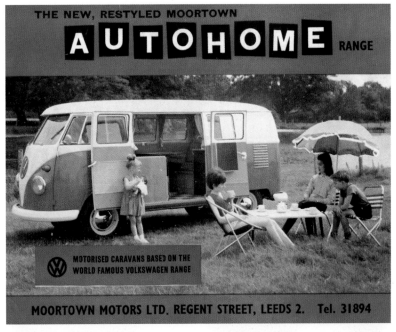

The cooker could be accessed from either side. A washing-up bowl was sited on the load door.

The Mark 5 featured a walk-through layout.

The front seat could make up into a child's berth, a lateral bunk behind it made another.

cool box fitted underneath. Microbus versions had a fluorescent light, whilst the Kombi version had a swan neck Tungsten light fitting. All woodwork was still in polished light oak, the table surfaces were faced with bird's eye Formica, whilst other unit door surfaces were picked out in olive green and all cupboards were fitted with chrome suitcase clasps.

RAISING THE ROOF

From 1960 Moortown models were also available with the option of a fitted Calthorp Elevating roof for an extra charge of £100. It was also still possible to order the hinged perspex roof ventilator up until 1963, when it was discontinued. From 1963 Moortown offered their own slimline pop-top elevating roof as an option instead of the Calthorp roof. Other optional equipment available included a lightweight awning or a complete tent awning known as the 'EM EM Lean to Annexe'. This was free standing and attached to the body by straps only, meaning no modifications to the bodywork. For the Mark 5 it was also possible to specify a special roof rack and all-weather cover to carry the spare, thus freeing up some interior space at the rear.

This 1965 Mark 5 features a rare Moortown elevating roof. The interior has been fully restored to original condition, although the cushion and curtain materials have been revamped to give a bright, cheerful look to complement the woodwork.

This 1965 model features the Moortown pop-top roof option.

Details like the lining of the cutlery drawer in green baize show the quality of the woodworking and fitments.

A wash bowl is stored in the load door cupboard; the door flaps down for a shelf.

This shows the wardrobe, bench seat, roof storage, pump tap and distinctive headlining.

The walk-through models were designated Mark 5. They featured a single seat behind the driver and the cooker cabinet by the load door.

The wardrobe door was an unusual shape; note additional storage at the rear side.

Oxley Coachcraft
VOLKSWAGEN SERIES

THE AIRFLOW H.T. AND RHEINLANDER MOTOR CARAVANS

The World at your Fingertips...

Oxley Volkswagen Series

THE AIRFLOW H.T.

THE RHEINLANDER

OXLEY COACHCRAFT
CRAVEN STREET, HOLDERNESS ROAD,
HULL, YORKS. ENGLAND Telephone 0482 20072

Oxley Coachcraft were a well-established caravan and coach-builder based in Hull, Yorkshire. By 1970 sales of motor caravans, especially on the VW base, were rising rapidly and, using their expertise, Oxley introduced two versions to the UK market, the Airflow HT and the Rheinlander. Both were based on Panel Vans, with the Airflow featuring a fixed high roof and the Rheinlander an elevating roof. Clearly, Oxley had checked out all the opposition and, whilst the layouts show influences from Devon and Dormobile, the combination of ideas and design made the Oxley a bit different. In particular, the materials, fittings and equipment were of a very high specification and the two very different layouts offered customers a good choice. All windows were aluminium framed and louvred, upholstery was quilted gold nylon, with the seats having rolled edges, walls and floors were vinyl clad and furniture was finished in simulated beige antelope hide, with tops and surfaces in teak laminate with white reverses. Teak pelmets were fitted above the curtain rails. An extra gas point for a gas fire was provided, as were a shaver point and two fluorescent lights. Extras included radio, fridge, electric water pump, cab centre seat, cab bunk and side awning. Versions could also be ordered with fixed roofs or LHD configuration.

THE AIRFLOW HT

This featured a low line high top with long louvred windows in each side. Bunks were fitted on either side. The kitchenette was arranged along the offside wall (like the Dormobile), with a two-ring cooker/grill, stainless steel sink unit with pump tap and drainer, large cool box and water container storage and cupboards. The table fixed to the middle of this unit to allow dinette style eating. A crockery cupboard was sited by the sliding door behind the passenger seat and there was a shelved wardrobe in the rear. Extra storage cupboards were fitted in the rear of the roof.

THE RHEINLANDER

This version had an elevating roof with a central opening roof light, windows in each side and two cab bunks. Seating was dinette style, with the sink unit sited at the end of the rear bench seat by the sliding door. A plastic-lined cool box was sited under the rear bench. The two-burner cooker/grill was fitted to a crockery cupboard behind the front passenger seat. At the rear were a shelved wardrobe, roof locker and deep drawers for the spare wheel and extra linen.

The 1953 Poba kit is perfect for this 1950 Panel Van.

Base units lock to the floor; here seating is arranged in a U shape.

The seats can also face forwards for travelling.

Batons to secure seating are permanently fixed. Note the immaculate interior paintwork.

The back of the side seat flips up to form a bunk berth.

Seat bases are moved into another position to form the full width double bed.

In the early 1950s Danish designer Poul Bader saw the potential being realized by Westfalia with their Camping Box conversion and designed an interior to fit all models of VW Bus, which he called POBA (after his name). It consisted of units that were designed as a series of interlocking boxes, locking to a floor template, which could be positioned to give a variety of layouts for travelling, dining and sleeping. The idea was based on the multi-purpose aspect of the Kombi, so that the vehicle could be a daily workhorse or load lugger, people carrier or Camper.

The early design, which ran through the fifties, basically consisted of three movable lockers with hinged seat bases for storage of bedding and so on (with bases and backs of upholstered deep foam rubber), and a table with folding legs. One ran across the back of the load compartment, one along the side wall facing the load

doors and the third could face forwards for travelling. For dining, this seat faced rearwards, making a three-sided rectangular seating arrangment around a folding table. The layout offered various sleeping arrangements – a single bunk along the side wall, a double bed or even a treble bed with a single bunk bed! There was also the option to make two children's berths in the front cab using the seat base and a bunk berth above it. It was also possible to order a pull-out awning or extra cupboards.

Everything locked to the floor for stability and safety. Once the basic fixing batons and floor were installed, it was only a matter of minutes to remove the furniture for outside use or for another use of the vehicle. In 1960 a Danish motor magazine heralded the POBA system with:

A new kind of camping is rapidly gaining interest abroad – the motorized

Camper. Here in Denmark motor caravans are opening up new possibilities for the traditional camping holiday. For a long time England has been at the forefront of pioneering caravans in Europe and nowadays they also seem to be at the forefront regarding camping vans. The best-known Campers are the Dormobile and of course the Westfalia, but now there is a new camping set-up from Denmark about to change things!

The Bus featured here is the oldest, most original VW Bus still in use today! It was built on 5 August 1950 on chassis number 20 1880, and left the factory on 8 August. It was delivered to J.C. Kornacker in Hildesheim, Germany, on 10 August. Kornacker was a hat maker and it was used as a delivery van right up until the early seventies. Apart from being a 'Barndoor Bus', with the distinctive features of a large engine lid and lack of peak over the front cab, this early example has rare, pre-November 1950-only features such as a rear badge, the spare wheel carried in vertical position in the engine bay and rain guttering around only three-quarters of the Bus. It was eventually acquired by Danish VW enthusiast Tonny Larsen, who set about a full bare metal restoration. He placed a 'wanted' ad in a camping magazine, asking for help in locating suitable camping furniture for a 1953 Bus (which he also owned), and to his surprise he received a call from someone who had furniture from a 1954 Danish conversion for a VW for sale! It turned out to be a very early POBA kit, which Tonny decided to fit in the Panel Van so that he could take the Bus to meetings and also use it for holidays. He drove the newly restored Bus from Denmark to debut at the vintage VW Bad Camberg Meet of 2003 where both the Bus and its interior caused quite a stir!

As can be seen in the photographs the interior is quite basic, but very flexible and roomy and is a rare vintage interior, in a rare vintage Bus.

By the mid-sixties the POBA Camper had developed to include more sophisticated camping facilities. It now consisted of two soft upholstered seats and bolster that converted into a 6.2ft by 4ft (190cm by 120cm) double bed. Under the seats was storage for cushions and blankets, clothes and so on. A single leg table, which could also be used outside, affixed to the side wall. Just inside the rear loading door was a wardrobe with hanging space, whilst behind the front seat was a cupboard for toiletries. The kitchen area was sited above the engine compartment at the rear and could be accessed from inside or outside the vehicle. A large pull-out drawer formed one half of the unit, whilst the two-ring cooker was housed in the other section. These were topped with removable Formica worktops. Side cupboards with hinge-up doors were fitted at each side of the area, making a complete kitchen. There was also a roof cupboard above the kitchen area.

The POBA Camping set was produced in seven different versions to give sleeping space for two, three and four adults and bunk beds for two children.

This lovely POBA Camper was built in August 1960 and exported to Sweden. It had one owner, who cared meticulously for it. Mechanically, the Bus retains all its factory specification except for a 6V to 12V conversion. The engine is a Volkswagen factory reconditioned 1200cc unit, and later spec tail lights and wing mirrors tell of a Bus cared for and used on a regular basis. It was resprayed at some point, having left the factory with the colour combination Grey over Mango Green. It has had a 1959 Eberspächer heater fitted post-factory for camping comfort. At some point in the early sixties it was then kitted out with the POBA kit, which was probably supplied in kit form for self-assembly, although the fitting is to a very high standard.

Mahogany laminated ply and yellow pine are all used in the construction, with clever elements of design incorporated into a functional leisure space. Storage space is maximized by the fitting of twin cupboards at the rear, allowing deep compartmentalized storage and space for a small gas cylinder to feed the stove. The stove is a cast-iron double burner which is sited under a laminated surface. The lid simply lifts off and the stove can be operated in situ. Beside the stove is a drawer for cutlery and other essential items. This drawer can either be pulled outwards towards the back of the vehicle (for cooking outside), or inside the vehicle if eating at the table. A rather useful feature of the POBA is the two preparation boards

This Swedish 1960 Bus has been fitted with the updated POBA kit.

This rear-facing view shows the full-length wardrobe and rear deck kitchen area with curtain screen.

The kitchen area features a larder, drawers and pull-out worktops.

The bed is made up by laying the table between the bench seats.

Shelves are angled to prevent items tipping out.

A small locker is sited at the side of the front bench seat.

The two-burner cooker can be accessed from inside as well as via the rear. The gas cylinder is housed in the adjacent cupboard.

that pull out from the rear of the vehicle, giving space for food to be prepared. These split in two, allowing close access to the stove at the same time. Directly above the stove and cutlery drawer area is a useful locker for pillows and other bedding. Again, this unit is finished in varnished mahogany ply with two brass slip bolts to hold it in place. Attention to detail and finish is of craftsman quality.

A small cupboard for belongings is located behind the bulkhead and provides a useful table top for such things as a radio or television. Directly opposite this cupboard is a spacious wardrobe with storage space below. The table sits into a low wooden box that doubles up as a bed support with ample storage space under each.

In order to lay the bed, two metal supports are placed across the rear seats to bridge the gap; one is at the furthest extremity and the other in the middle (the table support also acts as a support). The backs of both seats unclip from their upright position and are laid down flat. This allows ample lying space and also leaves room under the bed for additional storage (or for a child's bed).

A shelf above the rear seat is also provided, ideal for items that need to be close at hand and there are a number of handy hooks finishing off the interior of the van. The addition of a panelled pelmet above the curtains

signals the attention to detail and craftsmanship of the POBA Camper.

Now owned by Stuart McQuarrie and christened 'Dougal', the van can be seen travelling the Scottish Highlands. Stuart says of the POBA conversion, 'I think it stands out for its functionality, use of space and quality materials used in construction. Quality of construction and attention to detail sets the POBA out from the crowd.'

1968

The kit remained essentially the same for the new Bay Window Bus in 1968, except that an optional fridge or cool

box could replace the toiletry cupboard. Marketed as POBA Car furniture, kits were available to fit many makes of van and even cars. The POBA Campette version featured a new style of fibreglass elevating roof, which had a side-hinged section. Sleeping space could be extended by the use of a roof platform extension coupled with a tent awning or child's bunks. By 1972 the conversions were known as the POBA Auto Camper. Advertising claimed it took no more than thirty minutes to fit or remove the kit, and approximately five hours for initial basic installation of fixing sections and so on.

The 1972 POBA Auto Camper. Brochures were produced in several languages, including English and German, indicating the Camper's popularity outside Scandinavia.

Reimo is a well-established German firm, specializing in equipment for motor caravans and the associated leisure and camping lifestyle. Initially, during the 1970s, the firm offered a wide range of conversion kits and units, body parts and accessories, but by the 1980s were also producing fully fitted Campers. Known for build quality and finishing, Reimo conversions are still one of Europe's best-known motorhome converters. The T25 range consisted of the Alaska, with a sink/fridge/cooker unit by the sliding door, and the Florida, Yukon and Rhodos, which had the kitchenette arranged behind the driver. Reimo also supplied pop tops, front-hinged elevating roofs and high tops, as well as various styles of side window. The top of the range T4 conversion was known as the Miami, finished in very striking upholstery. Motor Caravan Conversions, based in Manchester, are now the franchised Reimo converter for the UK and they offer the full Reimo personal service, whereby a customer comes in and talks through requirements in detail before selecting from a range of alternative designs, options and accessories.

Riviera Motors were based in Oregon and were an official main VW dealership.

1965: MEETING THE DEMAND

Riviera Motors in Beaverton, Oregon, were the main distributor for Volkswagens in the Pacific north-west during the 1950s and 1960s. Camping was immensely popular in the Pacific north-west, and the Westfalia Campers were much in demand as they could get to places large RVs could not access. Demand was so great that the dealers couldn't get enough of them. Despite this, VWoA would only let dealers have Westies if they also took a certain number of commercials, but the dealers knew that commercials did not sell nearly as well as Campers! So, in the mid-sixties, Knute Qvale, owner of Riviera Motors, began talks with ASI Camper Conversions in Vancouver, Washington, about building their own camping conversion for Buses, based on the Westfalia interior. In 1965, the first of the new Riviera Campers hit the market. Interestingly, Riviera imposed a similar deal on their local VW dealer network as VWoA had done with them, by insisting that to get a certain number of Westfalia Campers, a certain number of Riviera conversions needed to be bought. Initial scepticism was soon dispelled once the build quality was seen and customers began to buy! No serial numbers or production numbers were ever kept on these Campers, so there is no way of knowing how many were made.

While Riviera made their business by taking new walk-through Panel Vans and converting them to Campers, it was not uncommon for a customer who already owned a van to have it kitted out by Riviera, which explains the apparent existence of pre-1965 Riviera conversions.

Like EZ and Sundial, the Riviera conversion was modelled closely on the Westfalia version, and even used some Westy parts. Apparently sales reps from Westfalia would check out what Riviera was doing and even used some of their ideas in next season's equipment!

RIVIERA CHARACTERISTICS

Riviera conversions were built primarily from walk-through Panel Vans; some non walk-through panel conversions and Kombi conversions do exist, but are few in number. Despite closely following the Westfalia designs, the Riviera had some unique and distinctive features.

The most obvious feature was the fitting of a long picture window along one side. Over the picture window is a piece of trim the length of the window and a chrome interior light. Single windows were fitted in each of the side loading doors. The windows were different from those fitted by EZ and Sundial in that they slide to open rather than flip open. Although some Campers have been found that use the flip-open type or even louvred versions, these are quite rare.

The interior headlining and panels were typically made from a lightly-stained birch wood and the interior colours offered included Blue/Teal, Red or White with matching table colours including Blue/Teal, White, or Yellow. The bed was a pull-out type with storage space underneath and the wardrobe was narrower, allowing for a wider bed. Behind the passenger seat was a cabinet housing an icebox, pump tap and water tank. No sink was fitted, but a Westy style flap-down table for a washing bowl was fitted on the side. A spice rack style storage unit was fitted on the rear load door.

Tents attached in two ways: by a 'slide rail' along the roof, similar to those used by Westfalia, or by two roof mounts that allowed the frame of the tent to hook to the body, similar to those used on Sundial Campers. While some Rivieras were outfitted with Sundial style tents, which attached using two fixed points along the roof, more Rivieras were built with a tent that utilized the slide rail. Tents frequently came in either red/white, blue/white, or green/white.

Some Rivieras came with a pop-top option. The top was made by Sportsmobile, Inc. of Elkhart, Indiana, and relatively few survive.

A long picture window, chrome light and wooden pelmet to hide the curtain rail are distinctive features of Riviera Campers.

An alternative style of picture window can be seen here, with louvres instead of sliding end sections.

The interior layout closely resembles Westfalia versions; the spice rack fitted to the rear door is often missing on surviving Buses.

Typical Riviera-style side tent awning.

The Camper shown here is a 1967 model based on a Pearl White Panel Van, and owned by Taylor and Amber Nelson. It was repainted in light mint green some time in the late 1970s, but the interior is virtually intact, apart from a spice rack storage unit which Nelson plans to fabricate himself. He has rebuilt the mechanicals and refitted new cab door panels and original style cab seats and is currently looking for an original style interior light and material to recover the rear bench seat/bed. When the Nelsons acquired the vehicle in 2003 they also found the original Coleman cooker and propane cylinder and the original jack, as well as a host of bits and pieces including a beach bucket, spade and camping chair!

This 1967 Riviera Camper is virtually intact, apart from the interior light and spice rack cabinet for the rear cargo door.

Slide-opening style windows are a distinctive Riviera feature. As most conversions were based on the Panel Van, aluminium-framed windows were riveted in.

The wardrobe and rear side cabinet were topped with a scalloped wood trim as a finishing detail. Wood headlining and an open rear shelf were also standard.

Flip-up side tables are fitted to the cooler cabinet and front cargo door.

Another distinctive Riviera feature is the long picture window. Note also the armrest cushion at the end of the bench seat.

Interior colours of tables and work surfaces were matched to upholstery colours.

No sink was fitted, just a pump tap. Worktops and tables are edged with chrome.

The picture window usually had sliding sections at either end.

The rear deck is used with a pull-out rear seat to form the double bed.

The Riviera licence plate surround was another standard feature.

Being based in Oregon, advertising brochures featured wild camping in forests and rugged mountains as a selling point.

1973: THE RIVIERA LINE

By 1972 Westfalia Campmobiles were again becoming very hard to buy in the US and by 1973 new Campmobiles were almost impossible to find. In response to this, Riviera and ASI launched a new generation of conversions called the Riviera Line, which featured three different elevating roof options.

The top of the range model was the Vista, which had a laminated fibreglass high top as standard. Sliding windows with screens were standard on the roof and sides. The dining area could be arranged U style at the rear, with a hanging closet, mains/battery fridge and sink unit along one side. A swivelling front seat was standard, as was mains electric and water hook-up. Woodwork was finished in cedar, and flooring was carpeted. The spare wheel was mounted on the front of the vehicle to create more room inside.

Plan 1 was the designation for the popular model. This was more like a Westy interior, with a single seat behind the front seat, a rear bench seat and table, a wardrobe and an icebox/toiletry cabinet inside the sliding door. The portable two-burner propane stove (propane has a lower freezing point than butane) was optional and could be mounted outside or used inside.

Three types of roof were available: the Vista high top, the Penthouse, which was a large pop-top about two-thirds of the Bus length, and the small Pop-Up Top as used on earlier Westfalias. Other optional equipment included: leisure battery, propane cooker, chemical toilet, child's hammock bunk, fridge, propane furnace heater, side tent, pull-out side awning, and even air conditioning!

The roof houses a full width double berth, with screened side 'windows' for light and ventilation.

This 1975 Riviera is owned by William Meyer, and has a Penthouse elevating roof, front-mounted spare wheel, mains hook-up and swage line striping.

The lower berth is also spacious. Note the roll-up door fitted to the side storage cupboard.

front cab with the back of the cab bench seat swinging up and supported by chains. Later models included a net to prevent a child falling out!

By far the biggest innovation, however, was the option of having a Calthorp Elevating Roof fitted. Calthorp Coachbuilders was a well established motor caravan concern, which offered conversions on marques such as Commer, Bedford and Standard. They developed the patent Calthorp Roof in 1958/59. They did not offer VW conversions; however, European Cars bought a franchise to allow them to fit the Calthorp roof to their newly developed Slumberwagen. As such, it is the first production elevating roof to be fitted to the VW Camper and beat Dormobile and Devon to it by two years!

In April 1960 the *Autocar* described it as 'One of the best and simplest of its kind, this elevating roof has a large, flexible metal panel which folds flat when lowered. The roof is rigid, draught-proof and waterproof whether raised or lowered and sliding windows for ventilation are included in the side pieces.' (Later reports, in 1962, on the new VW Dormobile with elevating roof were

less complimentary, finding condensation to be an annoying problem.)

There was also an option to have a cooker, with an integral gas bottle, allowing it to be lifted out of its unit and used outside. The Mark 2 also came complete with a four-person set of Meta ware cups, saucers, plates and cutlery.

Very few Slumberwagens were actually converted, and by 1965 it had stopped being produced completely.

The Bus featured here is rather special as not only does it have one of the very few Calthorp Roofs still in existence, it was also a one-off build by European Cars at the same time as they were developing the Slumberwagen.

In 1959 a young engineer returned to England with his new Austrian bride and they decided they wanted a Camper to do a Grand European Tour for their honeymoon trip. After checking out the Westfalia models on offer at the time, they realized they wanted something more luxurious, with a more sophisticated cooker and a heater! One feature the wife specifically wanted was a 'proper' sink instead of the washing bowl/toiletry unit found on Westies. They also

wanted an elevating roof as the husband was quite tall and had checked out the Dormobiles on offer, none of which were yet VW based. Eventually they came across the firm of European Cars, who were carrying out conversions on Bedfords and Commers, and who offered the 'Calthorp Elevating roof' with their models. Currently under design was a VW based version and it is probable the young couple saw early versions of the forthcoming Slumberwagen at the works, but it still did not quite meet their desire for luxury. Instead, they negotiated with the company for a tailor-made version of the forthcoming Slumberwagen. They wanted bigger side windows than were fitted to the standard Kombi, so opted for a Panel Van as the base model and had special larger sliding windows installed that matched the style of window in the Calthorp Roof, using an up/down arrangement. All the cabinet work was based on their own specifications, with storage space in just about every imaginable place! There are cupboards above the side windows below the roof, and side and corner units all with drawers, compartments or dividers. Even the front cab

This Bus was converted by Calthorp in 1959, as a special order, whilst they were developing the prototype Slumberwagens.

was reworked to give extra storage space behind and under the seat. Other distinctive features included a period radio, barometer, fan, luxury wall clock and an exterior light mounted above the rear side window.

The finished Camper actually cost twice as much as the standard Westfalia, but the owners considered it worth the expense. After travelling round Europe in 1961/62, they settled in Austria, where the Camper remained in use by the family until 1996, when it was stored before ending up back in England via a German collector in 2002.

So this is a unique VW Camper. Produced by European Cars whilst they were designing their Slumberwagen, it features an individually tailored, superbly crafted interior and is also the only known surviving example of a VW fitted with a Calthorp Roof; as such it is a rare beauty indeed.

The Calthorp roof has a low profile when folded down.

The sliding side windows were built to match the style of those in the roof. Note the longer window in the rear sides.

Interior layout was functional and practical, with a very modern-looking sink unit.

The cooker unit features slide-out storage and a bottle compartment that are years ahead of their time.

There is even a cargo net behind the front bench seat back!

More storage in the roof cupboards.

Wood panelling and storage, storage and more storage!

Even the spaces behind and under the cab bench seat are utilized.

The rear is designed for storing suitcases or picnic hampers.

From 1955 VW Transporters were assembled by South Africa Motor Assemblers in Uitenhage, from CKD (Completely Knocked Down) kits supplied mainly by Hanover. In 1956 VW took controlling interest, and the plant was eventually renamed Volkswagen of South Africa in 1966. Camping conversions were usually Westfalia Campmobiles, again supplied in kit form from Germany for assembly, though sometimes copies of parts were sourced locally; however, in the sixties CKD kits were also imported from VW Brazil, which accounts for some unusual variants as parts from various model years were used simultaneously in Brazilian-built Buses. On South African Buses a cyclone air filter was usually standard, as were front and rear reflectors fitted below the lights.

The vehicle featured here is somewhat unusual in that it was built in 1966 but has a very distinctive and different arrangement from the usual 1960s Westfalia Campmobiles, and is nothing like SO 42/44. This is the only known example of this type of conversion in Europe, and the only one known to survive anywhere in such immaculate condition.

The South African spec reflectors can clearly be seen and the Bus also originally had factory-fitted tinted windscreens. Unusually it has extra twin fresh air ventilation fans in the roof. One other interesting aftermarket South African feature is the addition of extra cooling vents, behind the standard vents, each with a chrome cover that can be flapped open to allow more cooling air to be forced into the engine bay. The model also exemplifies the 'combination of features from various model years' found on South African Buses supplied by VW Brazil, in this case a pre-1966 tailgate with post-1966 bumpers, whilst behind the fish-eye indicators are the pressings to take earlier style bullet indicators. It also has 15in wheels, instead of the 14in versions used after 1964. Another unusual South African-only feature is that the front bulkhead is smooth.

As it was built for the newly named VW South Africa, the camping interior follows its own design instead of the Campmobile copy route, though it is not known if this interior went into full production; by 1969 the new Bay Window Campmobiles were available to order.

The dinette style of two bench seats round a fold-down table was added to with storage/cupboard units and worktops at either end of the seats, by the loading doors. The front unit has a storage cupboard with flap-down opening door, on top of which is a double door storage cupboard, topped with, and fronted by, a worktop in laminate to match the table. The rear unit is almost identical but not as deep, and has an evaporation cool box sited in the base. At the rear is a large deep drawer, with twin door side cupboards facing each other. A small toiletry cabinet is mounted on the rear load door. The vinyl headlining has been retained, but all interior panels are wood ply and the high quality cabinet work is finished in light oak. A cooker was not supplied as

standard and there was no pumped water supply.

1969: THE KAMPMOBILE

With the advent of the Bay Window model, in October 1969 VWSA launched its own version of the Campmobile, designated as the Kampmobile. It was assembled at the Uitenhage plant and designed to be both Camper and people carrier, retaining the eight seater capacity. Based on the bulkhead model, it used Westfalia equipment and parts (or copies of them) and was very similar to the SO 69 series marketed in Europe. The Westfalia front-hinged elevating roof, with an integral roof rack at the rear, was fitted as standard and the model could sleep three adults and two children, with a cab hammock bunk supplied as standard. A free-standing tent awning was available as an option. The rear bench seat pulled out to form a full width double bed and, behind the passenger seat, just inside the sliding door, was a 2.6cu ft icebox. Water from the melting ice was collected in a drip tray and drained off outside the vehicle. A 6gal (27ltr) water tank was sited in the rear of the cabinet, which also housed a sink, pump tap and cutlery drawer, and had two flap-up table tops for kitchen workspace on the sliding door side, along with a small open storage shelf/cupboard. A dinette table was located between the two bench seats and a cargo net was slung in the roof at the rear. Also sited in the rear was a wardrobe with a mirror and linen closet. All interior panelling was birch plywood. A clip-on mosquito net and two louvred windows (one on either side) were also standard. The 1600cc engine was beefed up with a higher compression ratio of 7.7:1, instead of the usual 6.6:1 of the standard Kombi.

1974: THE KOMBI KAMPER

In 1974 a restyled version, called the Kombi Kamper, was introduced, at a much lower price than the previous Kampmobile. No elevating roof was fitted and equipment was fairly basic. Designed to seat five/six, it came with storage lockers, full length wardrobe, and fold-down table between two bench seats. The rear bench doubled as a pull-out bed, and a child's cab bunk was supplied. Light woodgrain panelling was fitted throughout the rear (living) section. An icebox and water storage were housed in a kitchen cabinet inside the sliding door behind the front passenger seat, with a Formica worktop. Options included a two-way gas/electric fridge, full length roof rack and large or small tent awnings.

THE JURGENS AUTO VILLA

Jurgens Caravans were based at Kempton Park in the Transvaal and were an established caravan and motor caravan conversion business. In 1973 they constructed a coach-built motor caravan conversion on the VW base, which was designated the Auto Villa. This conversion was way ahead of its time with luxury fitments like a built-in shower; even today it stands alongside modern coach-built Campers and RVs.

The Luton top over the cab is a distinctive Jurgens feature, not found on the Karmann version.

Jurgens applied their established designs and building processes to a 2ltr Microbus base, with the caravan section constructed from extruded aluminium frames and aluminium cladding to give strength without excessive weight. Polystyrene insulation was fitted throughout and all the interior panelling was from Taiwan hardwood veneer, chosen because of its warp-resistance property. The inside height was 6ft 3in (1.9m), giving a feeling of spaciousness, while the walk-through cab made the whole vehicle feel self-contained and snug.

Above the front cab was a Luton extension, which housed a double berth and was reached via a ladder. The interior layout was similar to that of a modern caravan, with dinette seating for four to six people at the rear, in a U shape round a removable table. This lay down to form a double or two single berths. Along one side behind the cab was the washroom, equipped with mirror, toiletry cabinet, washbasin, footbath and shower. There was room in this area to include a chemical toilet. By the side of the washroom area an 85ltr gas/electric fridge was fitted.

Opposite this was the kitchenette, complete with sink, two-burner hob, grill and overhead cupboards. A full set of crockery and cutlery, bearing the Jurgens crest, was also supplied. Next to the kitchenette was the side door with fitted mosquito screen and slide-down window.

A 12V electric pump drew water for washing or the kitchen sink from four 2.2gal (10ltr) storage bottles. Roller blinds were fitted to all windows, carpeting to all floor areas and an external sun canopy was also standard. A free-standing tent awning was available optionally. To cope with fuel consumption and extend the driveable range (especially in the South African wilderness) two 12.3gal (56ltr) fuel tanks were fitted on either side of the engine compartment, giving a potential 560 miles (900km) range.

By 1979 over 1,000 units had been built and, in a road test report, *Car South Africa* commented, 'This is South Africa's most unusual vehicle; a combination of car and caravan, and a touring vehicle par excellence. It is not everyone's idea of motoring, especially given its price, but as a specialized vehicle in a specialized field it is a world beater.'

The Jurgens Auto Villa was a pioneer in the motor caravan field and a major influence on the design of motorhomes and RVs. In the mid 1970s Karmann Karosserie acquired the rights to build a version under licence. This led to the manufacture of the famous, and perhaps better known, Karmann Mobile and, subsequently, the Karmann Gipsy, which were manufactured in both Germany and Brazil (*see* Chapter 20).

Very little is known about the company Sport Kocijan, except that they were based in Vienna and produced craftsman-built camping interiors in the early sixties. The interior featured here was originally fitted in a 1962 Austrian Samba, and was rescued by Andy Barrott, who then fitted it into his 1961 Samba. It is completely original and in excellent condition.

Like many conversions it was designed to be easily removable, allowing the Bus to be used for other purposes. Interestingly, it resembles the layout of the Westfalia SO 44, but actually predates it by several years.

Designed to fit bulkhead models, the furniture consists of a long unit behind the bulkhead, with a large capacity full length wardrobe, with hanging rail, sited at the end opposite the load doors. Yellow Formica topping on the unit complements the light oak woodwork, and the build quality is excellent. The main unit has a large, shelved storage cupboard, with a smaller section by the load doors housing the cutlery drawer, and two storage cupboards. The cutlery drawer comes complete with wooden cutlery holder; even this has dove-tailed joints!

A wooden bench seat neatly converts to a double bed by pulling out the base, folding down the legs and laying the seat back onto the frame. The two seat cushions lay down and meet the large cushion over the engine compartment to form a roomy bed. For travelling, the cushions are held in place with material straps that match the grey fabric – not the most practical method of securing them! The bench seat is not quite full width and a wooden stay, fixed on the end, folds down to keep secure those items carried on the floor at the end of the bench seat.

The interior came complete with a boxed, unused, 1961 Flaga Piccolo two-burner cooker, which sits on top of the gas bottle, though it is not known if this was provided as part of the camping kit.

This 1961 Samba has one of only two known examples of this interior to survive intact.

The interior features bulkhead cabinets and a full height wardrobe, like the later Westfalia SO 44.

Cabinet work was hand-built to a very high standard; even the cutlery drawer uses dove-tailed joints.

Period Piccolo cooker shows modern minimalist design styling.

Cushions are held in place by straps. Note the swivel peg, at the end of the seat base, to secure items stored in the space at the end of the seat. No separate table was provided.

To make the bed remove the seat covers, pull out the frame from the rear deck, fold down the legs and use seat boards for the base to make a neatly engineered high level bed.

Sportsmobile

FAMILY WAGON • CAMPER • UTILITY VEHICLE Switch from one to the other in less than one minute — arrange furnishings to fit your activities. Luxurious styling, highest quality materials and craftsmanship assure maintenance-free year-round enjoyment. Optional free-standing canopy and side-walls add a room in minutes, to hold your campsite or to use at home. Canopy top may be left off for a private sunroom. For travel, tent rolls up in travel case and secures to vehicle roof brackets.

TRAVEL EQUIPMENT CORPORATION
SPORTSWAGON CONVERSIONS DIVISION
406 Jay Dee Road, Elkhart, Ind. / 945 West 190th St., Gardena, Cal.

'The Family Wagon Camper for Volkswagens'.

Sportsmobile were an established RV company, based in Andrews, Indiana, with a West Coast branch situated in Gardena, California. Like many other US outfits, they began developing a VW Camper conversion around 1965/66. The conversion was designed to be fully removable in just a few minutes, in order to exploit the multi-purpose nature of the Transporter.

Conversions were available for walk-through and bulkhead models; behind the cab seats were a single seat, middle jump seat and a unit by the load door that housed the icebox cabinet and a mirror. A folding down seat was sited behind the icebox for use when the icebox was removed. At the top of this was a family glass holder and glasses (similar in concept to the Westy SO 32). A flap-down table was affixed to the side wall. The rear bench seat was a pull-out bed at engine shelf height, with a hanging space by the load door (a wardrobe bag was provided). Another unit, containing two water jugs, a wash-basin and a pump, was sited on the rear load door. The door of the unit flapped down to act as a shelf for using the two-ring LPG burner. At the rear was an open roof shelf above the engine with a side linen/storage cupboard opposite the spare wheel carrying space (though often the spare was carried on the optional roof rack). The inclusion of a mains 110V hook-up with 35ft cable shows Sportsmobile's RV background! Panel Van conversions had louvred windows as standard, but these were optional for Kombi and Microbus versions. Walls, ceiling and door panels were laminated with Monsanto Ultra vinyl and all panels and exposed edges were trimmed with polished alumini-um and matched extruded plastic.

Authorized VW dealers would fit a Sportsmobile kit in less than five hours, but DIY versions were also available. An adapter kit meant that pre-1964 models could also be fitted with the Sportsmobile camping interior.

Options included a pop-top roof, roof rack, free-standing sun canopy, side walls, screened window and a floor for a sun canopy (which could be erected without the canopy roof for a private sunroom!), a cab hammock bunk, chemical toilet (stored in the single seat behind the driver in its own compartment for inside or outside use), a vinyl weatherproof roof rack case, Dana heater, side window screens and a mosquito screen for the rear when the tailgate was open.

The same principles and build quality applied from 1969 when they continued to offer full conversions based on Bay Window VW Panel Vans, Kombis and Microbuses, which were fully removable, allowing the vehicle to be used for other purposes. The conversions were also offered in kit form, or could be fitted to customers' existing vehicles. The kits to fit pre-1967 Buses were still available, however.

The versatility of the camping kit was part of Sportsmobile's marketing strategy, with brochures referring to, 'another practical feature of the Sportsmobile is that you can leave the camping furnishings at home – such as the wardrobe, table, bed mattress, front seat and icebox cabinet. Everything snaps out in a minute – and when removed, the Sportsmobile is still completely finished inside – no bare metal areas showing.'

The new style optional elevating roof was Sportsmobile's own design. It was a pop-top now running the full length of the load area and called the Penthouse. The spare wheel was mounted on the front and three louvred windows were fitted to Panel Vans, or two on the Kombi. As well as a bench and single seat round a table, a removable icebox cabinet, which included a sink, water pump and 5gal (22.7ltr) tank, was sited behind the front passenger seat. Fixed to this, by the sliding door, was a small, shelved storage cupboard, with a door that flapped up to make a shelf. The door

could be fully swung up to reveal a vanity mirror fixed to the back. The shelf was ideal for using a small camping cooker (not provided), or for a washing bowl. The rear bench seat was adjustable to two positions and also formed a rock-and-roll pull-out style bed with a steel frame.

An optional wardrobe unit was sited at the end of the rear bench seat. The standard equipment was a vinyl removable hanging wardrobe bag, which could be hung in the same position. There was also an open storage roof shelf above the engine compartment. Woodwork was finished in medium oak, scratch-resistant laminate and seats were covered in Naugahyde light colour vinyl, which harmonized with crease-resistant check curtains. The floor covering was cushioned vinyl that was both indent-resistant and hot grease-proof. The

ceiling and walls were all clad in light vinyl panels, with laminate trim to match the cabinets. Mains hook-up was standard.

Optional equipment included a ladder for the Penthouse roof, side tent awning, roof rack, small pop-top roof, flush chemical toilet, cab centre seat, cab hammock bunk, cab divider curtains, Dana petrol heater, gangway seat stool, cab armrests and rear, side and cab window screens.

As well as being fitted on their own Campers, the Sportsmobile Penthouse roof was bought and fitted both by private individuals and other conversion companies. Even VWoA offered it as an option on their own Westfalia style Camper in the early 1970s.

Sportsmobile continues to produce RV vehicles today, and produced Campers and multi-purpose vehicles on both the T25 and T4 platforms.

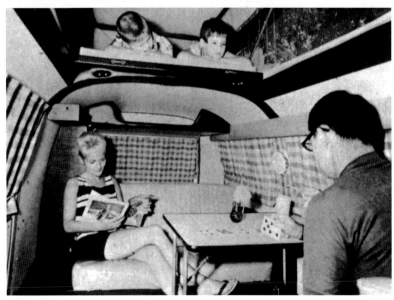

The Penthouse top was used by VWoA in their 1970 Campmobiles and featured a slide-out bed, not bunks.

The 1966 brochure cover shows the fringed, striped Sundial tent.

The bed used the rear deck and all panelling was in wood ply.

It also shows a Riviera style wooden pelmet over optional bottom opening windows.

Multi-purpose use has always been a feature promoted by converters.

In the 1960s US dealerships had problems in meeting demands for Westfalia Campers – orders were not easily placed and often they would have to take what was delivered! Many Westfalias were actually brought into the country via the Tourist Export programme whereby individuals (usually US Forces personnel) picked up their vehicle from the factory and arranged shipping to the US. Sundial Campers were based in California and, like EZ and Riviera, produced a camping interior that was modelled closely on the Westfalia versions, and, like the others, even used Westy parts or close copies of them, as can be seen on the Sundial featured here. If a customer could not buy a Westfalia, then a Camper that had similar, recognizable, features was an attractive alternative. Some people jokingly refer to these Campers as 'Westfakias', but the build quality was usually very good and all had their own unique features.

Sundial conversions were usually based on the standard Panel Van (which was more readily obtainable) and then kitted out with five louvred opening side windows (six if the wardrobe was omitted). The most distinctive and obvious features of a Sundial Camper were the five louvred windows, which were cut into the Panel Van, and based on the Westfalia louvred version. However, Kombis and Microbuses were also converted. Whilst the Panel Van conversion had five side windows, the Kombi/Microbus base retained all six windows – in this case one non-louvred window remained, as it was inside the wardrobe space. There was also an option to have single pane opening windows hinged at the top. The windows were fitted with fly screens as standard.

The walls and ceiling were panelled in platinum ash plywood (like Westies), with the option of a similar finish for the cab doors, and vinyl flooring was fitted throughout. White vinyl seat covers were fitted over the cab seats and the other upholstery was from a choice of six colours with matching or contrasting corduroy curtains hung on brass rods. The bed was a Z-bed easy action style, similar to rock-and-roll beds (and quicker to operate than the standard Westy design). The furniture was well made in matching ash with anodized aluminium mouldings to protect the edges. Although closely modelled on a Westy, the Sundial has some interesting, and unique, variations.

Opposite the rear wheel storage space at the back is a sliding door cabinet with fitted shelving. The left loading door is fitted with a large cupboard for crockery and so on, with either slatted shelves or a pull-down door doubling as a work or table space. This is topped by a spice rack with circular holes for containers or cups. The right loading door has a flap-down Formica shelf, on which the cooker (either Benz-o-matic or Coleman) stands when camp is set up. The cooker is stored under one of the bench seats when not in use. Looking inside on the left is a large wardrobe with mirror with a bench seat (which pulls out as the bed) and a magazine rack at the far end. There are three sizes of folding tables, which fit to the side wall and hinge upwards or lie flat against it when not in use. Above the rear seat is a ceiling-mounted storage

A 1965 Sundial Conversion, with fitted roof rack.

area. The front bulkhead of Panel Vans was cut out to make a walk-through cab version, with a single seat on one side and a large cupboard housing the sink, fridge (or cool box) and water container on the other. This 12gal (54.5ltr) water container is sealed in a wooden housing, which separates from the base unit and lifts out for easy filling. The circular sink is fitted with a removable chopping board and the unit also has a cutlery drawer above the fridge. White vinyl seat covers are fitted to the cab seats.

A tent awning was also standard and is very distinctive with its bright striping and white fringing. Options included a roof rack and ladder, truck style large side mirrors, a roof vent (similar to the Westy roof hatch), a side step, which folded flat under the vehicle, and a child's hammock for the front cab area. A Benz-o-matic fridge was also available instead of the standard icebox. A folding toilet with Cabana tent could also be supplied.

The model pictured here is owned by Dave Lloyd. Built in November 1965, it was supplied as a walk-through Kombi finished in Dove Blue. Interestingly, it had originally been factory fitted with middle and rear seats + wood trim and had six opening pop-out side windows, though these were obviously removed, probably by the converters.

In order to recreate the California look, the Bus has been lowered and fitted with SA Sprintstars. A missing Sundial badge and tap were sourced from the US via the Internet as were some truck mirrors; from drillings on the body it is clear that the Bus originally had these. The planned stainless steel air scoops for the rear cooling vents and chrome safaris will add to that California look. These will clip on to save drilling the bodywork. US spec bumpers with overriders and towel rails are also being sourced, as the current bumpers mix slash end (pre-1966) and pointed end (post-1966), but have all the drillings for overriders, which must have been removed at some time. The Bus has been resprayed at some point with a two-tone paint scheme, but the blue is not a true Dove Blue match as it is more grey-blue than blue-grey.

A Coleman petrol cooker could be mounted on the front loading door shelf.

The distinctive Sundial sink/fridge/water container cupboard. Unusually, the sink cover/chopping board is still in place, but a replacement original tap unit had to be sourced via the Internet.

The detachable free-standing water container makes for easy filling. Note the interesting burn marks on the door-mounted cooker flap!

The door-mounted crockery cupboard is similar to the Westfalia version but has a flap-down door and spice/mug rack.

Wooden panelling and headlining throughout give that 'camping in a cabin' feel.

115

A sliding door reveals ample additional storage.

The period Coke bottle radio works (sometimes) by rotating its base.

The main table folds against the sidewall when not in use.

Curtains used a brass rail, not sliders.

Sundial fitted white vinyl seat covers to the cab seats, as can just be seen here.

The maker's plate.

The original Sundial badge is very hard to find if missing.

Note that the rear window here (behind the wardrobe) is standard, not louvred, as this conversion was based on a Kombi.

Truck mirrors were original features on this Bus and these have recently been refitted to restore the period look.

The California licensing plate approving the vehicle.

Louvred windows all round are a distinctive feature of the Sundial conversion.

Syro, based near Darmstadt, was another German camping equipment manufacturer and camping converter, which offered a comprehensive range of conversions for several marques, including Ford and Mercedes, as well as Volkswagen. The name Syro came from Sybille and Rolf Koch, who founded the company in the early 1970s. By 1978 Syro had at least fifteen shops in West Germany and one in Austria. Quality was very good and customers liked being able to select from single units or packages to fit out a vehicle for their specific needs.

This cutaway view shows one style of several possible layouts.

All components were available in kit form and a comprehensive guide showed how to assemble all the various pieces and combinations. The base plan, VW 2, had dinette style seating, with a cooker sited at the top and back of the single seat by the sliding door and a sink unit in the seat base. Option VW 3 had a fridge/cooker/sink unit by the sliding door, instead of a seat, to which the table could attach for outside use. Various other packaged options were available, including a layout featuring the cooker and sink unit running across the front bulkhead to meet a wardrobe. There were also pop-top roofs (using Syro's own design) and front-hinged elevation roofs (using the Westfalia version) available as options, as well as a massive roof tent and awning.

In addition to supplying kits and components, Syro also offered new conversions with the same range of layouts and options, until they ceased trading in around 1985.

The massive roof tent and side awning, made by Syro, are shown here.

A comprehensive handbook gave full detailed instructions for DIY assembly.

Syro designed kits for a range of marques and offered a variety of layouts.

The Autohomes Kamper featured a rigid side elevating roof and a well-appointed interior.

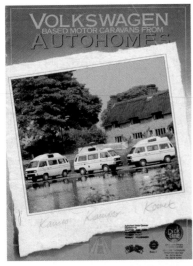

By the start of the 1980s Campers were becoming much more luxurious and well appointed, in response to changes in consumer lifestyles. Levels of luxury and fitments were offered that were above that found in many homes! The humble VW Camper began to transform into something very different to meet this change and the new T25 base quickly established itself as a popular model for many motor caravan manufacturers in the UK, with most producing at least one VW conversion in their range. Whilst T25 Campers produced by major players such as Devon, Westfalia and Auto-Sleeper have been covered separately, it is not possible, within the scope of this book, to cover all the T25 camping conversions offered; however, some of the more popular UK models are described below.

AUTOHOMES

Autohomes have always been a major player in the motorhome business and their T25 range came in three versions: Kameo, Kamper and Komet. The interiors for all three models were essentially the same; it was the roof styles that were the key difference.

The Kameo was a two-person conversion, with the option of a cab bunk. It featured an aerodynamic low-line roof with opening windows, roof light and integral roof rack. The roof also featured pull-out storage units for bottles, glassware and crockery. A swivelling front passenger seat was standard.

The Kamper had an elevating roof with a double bed, meaning four adults could sleep in comfort. A unique feature of the roof was that it had rigid sides, one of which could flap down for extra ventilation or a private grandstand! For travelling, it could seat six with a multi-position, sliding, swivelling and reclining seat behind the front passenger. This could face forwards for travelling or be used as a single or double seat for dining. There was also a mobile stool storage box between the front seats.

The Komet was a four-berth high top, with a double bed in the roof. The roof had a multi-directional opening roof light and two high-level, opening, double-glazed windows. It came with a stainless steel ladder and roof rack. Both front seats were swivel seats and an extra table was supplied for use, with these, in the cab. Crockery and a flush toilet were also standard. Options included TV, melamine crockery (Kameo and Kamper), leisure battery, blown air heating, rear spare wheel carrier, making the single seat with the Kamper easily removable.

COUNTRY CAMPERS

This was a small firm based in Fareham, Kent, specializing in the fitting of windows, high tops or elevating roofs to vehicles, as well as carrying out conversions to private vehicles or supplying fully fitted Campers. The classic late Devon Moonraker arrangement was followed with a cooker, fridge, sink unit and storage under the windows with a wardrobe at the rear. A single box seat, which could house an optional Porta Potti, was sited just inside the sliding door behind the front passenger seat. Cabinets were finished in white or cream melamine and fabrics for seats and curtains were chosen by the customer from a wide range of stock.

EURO MOTOR CAMPERS (EMC)

This was another firm that specialized in furniture kits and which manufactured high tops and elevating roofs for a range of vans such as VW, Mercedes, Renault, Bedford and Ford. Their high top roof was called the Town and Country. They also made high tops to fit Bay Window VWs. The interiors offered lots of storage cupboards, with distinctive plastic trim round all doors and edges. There were seven packages available, from just windows and high top, to a fully fitted out conversion. EMC also built interiors to customer requirements.

LEISUREDRIVE

The conversion firm Leisuredrive, of Salford, Manchester, is still a well-established converter supplying DIY kits. Their T25 conversion was called the Crusader. The interior layout was very similar to that pioneered by the 1978 Moonraker, with cooker, fridge, sink and storage unit under the windows and a wardrobe in the rear. The single seat behind the passenger was a fold-down unit/Porta Potti and a front passenger swivel seat was optional. Three roof styles were offered: a side-hinged elevating roof; a Lo-Line High Top; and the Mark 3 Hi-Line High Top. The cabinet work was finished in wood-look melamine.

ADVANCED 'SPORT 6'

The Advanced 'Sport 6' conversion was carried out by Advanced Bus in Derby and was designed to appeal to those who wanted to combine Minibus and Camper in one versatile, but very comfortable, vehicle. The layout is based on the Day Van design and the interior is fully insulated and carpeted, including the ceiling. For travelling, the swivelling front pair of seats (complete with head and raising armrests) can face forwards so that the interior is arranged like a Minibus. However, it is also equipped for use as a Camper with a sink, single hob cooker, rock-and-roll bed, rear bench seat and front swivel seats, which can be arranged dinette fashion round a removable centre table. Also included are reading lamps for all seats, foot well lamps and twin sunroofs. This particular model also has factory-fitted twin sliding doors, big bumpers and central locking, whilst the high-level brake light was added by Advanced. The conversion was ordered by the Trust VW dealership in Leeds in 1991, which supplied the base Kombi. The first owner saw this T25 in Trust VW's showroom as he drove past. He bought it from the showroom straight away and the original paperwork shows that Advanced Bus charged Trust Motors £4,317, for the conversion work, on an invoice dated the day before the registration of the Bus. The

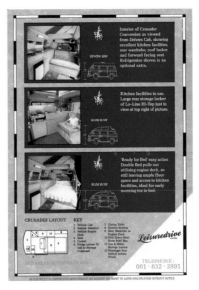

119

total cost of the Bus new and on the road was £15,312. The owner kept it in immaculate condition and when current owner Mick Mclaren bought it in April 2002 it had only clocked 6,000 miles (9,650km)!

The vehicle was in excellent condition and required very little work, although Mick had the front end resprayed to get rid of stone chips, and touched in new paint in an area that had faded slightly, apparently from being too near the heater in the previous owner's garage! Since acquiring the Bus, Mick has developed his own look, with a range of period accessories and custom parts including factory alloys, which have been fully refurbished, a dash rev counter, Gene Berg short shifter kit, grille spoiler, jail bars, carat lamp surrounds, full length lower grill, front spoiler fog lamps, clear indicator lenses, new curtains and specially designed sunroof blinds. The Bus has been lowered 45mm on Spax progressively wound sport springs, which Mick says has made it handle better.

Future plans include bigger wheels and a more powerful engine, but what Mick really likes about the Sport 6 conversion is its versatility and being able to use it for work, shopping, school runs and as a load hauler.

The table is pedestal mounted.

The 1991 Sport 6 combined luxury people carrier with weekend Camper.

The double door model allows for easy access from either side – very safe for dropping off the children!

Twin swivel seats, with arm and headrests offer flexible seating for dining.

For travelling the seats face forwards.

Twin sunroofs let in plenty of light.

The rock-and-roll bed is easy to operate and spacious.

A sink unit and tap are sited at the end of the rear bench seat.

The dealership badge and Sport 6 logo are fixed at the rear.

WENTWORTH MOTOR CARAVANS

Wentworth were a small family-run business operating from Egham in Surrey. Specializing in VW conversions, they usually built to order, taking about eight weeks to carry out the conversion. They also carried a small stock of conversions on second-hand vehicles and would source vehicles to customer requirements. By converting used vehicles, a fully appointed VW motorhome became a more affordable and attractive option.

A Wentworth HiTop roof with 6ft (1.8m) roof bed was standard and all furniture was quality built and finished in oak. Behind the driver was a single seat with the sink, electric water pump, fridge, cooker and storage unit running under the windows. A wardrobe was sited in the rear. A bench seat/rock-and-roll bed ran across the rear and another single seat was sited behind the passenger, with a table between them. The interior was well-appointed. Standard equipment included dash table/tray, waste water tank, removable 9gal (41ltr) fresh water tank, louvred window with screen, leisure battery and a barbecue. Options included TV, water heater, swivel seats, mains hook-up, cycle, ski or surfboard racks, sound system and side awning or tent. One rather unusual option was to have a shower fitted where the single seat behind the driver was sited!

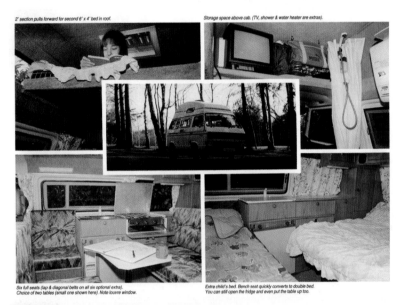

2' section pulls forward for second 6' x 4' bed in roof.

Storage space above cab. (TV, shower & water heater are extras).

Six full seats (lap & diagonal belts on all six optional extra). Choice of two tables (small one shown here). Note louvre window.

Extra child's bed. Bench seat quickly converts to double bed. You can still open the fridge and even put the table up too.

In the late 1970s the German firm, Teca Reisemobile GmbH, offered a series of camping kits designed for the VW Bus. Kits could be supplied in DIY form, or could be fitted to new or used vehicles, and it was also possible to specify options within each kit. Models featured fixed roof, pop top, front-hinged elevating and high top roofs. They were uninspiringly called after the Greek Alphabet for differentiation – Alpha was the basic no-frills model with basically just a bed, while Sigma was the fully fitted high roof model. Four examples of the layouts are shown here.

Einrichtung GAMMA

Einrichtung GAMMA S

Einrichtung DELTA

Einrichtung SIGMA

Originating in the USA, whose inhabitants have a long-standing love of the Pick-Up Truck, the demountable camping unit enabled a vehicle to be freed for other workhorse use or to act as family runabout whilst the unit remained at camp, with the front supported by fold-down legs. The idea is rooted in having a portable caravan body which sits 'piggy back' onto the flatbed, and quickly caught on in the US. Most companies manufactured a base unit that could be used with any Pick-Up Truck model; very few offered a specific VW conversion.

The idea never really caught on in the same way in Europe; however, one German company, Tischer, did successfully specialize in fully fitted, demountable cabins for the VW single and double cab Pick-Up Truck. Interior finishing was to a very high standard, with shower units and fully fitted kitchens coupled with luxurious upholstery. They started converting in the 1970s and are still successfully producing models today.

The first Vikings had fixed or pop-top roofs.

The dinette could quickly lay out into L-shaped seating.

At night the Bus transformed into a boudoir!

The well-appointed Viking kitchen was sited in the rear.

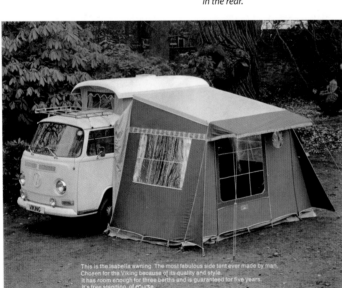

The optional Isabella free-standing awning created even more space.

'This is an outstanding design, quite the most original and successful ever on a Volkswagen.'
Camping Caravan Weekly,
November 1972.

The Viking conversion is best known for its distinctive elevating roof. When travelling, the Viking looks like any elevating roof VW Camper, but, when parked up, the difference becomes immediately obvious in that the roof is huge! It is actually combined with an overhanging side tent extension, giving masses of headroom and space for adults to sleep comfortably in the roof!

THE VOLKSWAGEN VIKING

The Viking was launched in 1970 and produced by Motorhomes of Berk-hampstead, Hertfordshire. Based on Panel Vans, they initially offered a fixed roof with an optional two-thirds pop-top elevating roof for the middle and rear section.

The spacious interior layout, however, differed from its contemporaries, and advertising of the time highlighted this with:

Viking. So much more than a Volkswagen. Viking is an entirely new concept in motor caravan design and its versatile use of space, ingenious design and superb quality put it ahead of the field – in every field. There's room for everything in a Viking. Room for lounging and dining. Room for cooking and loving. And a separate room for the children.

Bench seats faced each other to seat four or five, with an optional portable gas or electric chest fridge sited behind the front passenger by the sliding door. A table could be fixed in the centre or, alternatively, an L-shaped settee could be formed by positioning the rear bench under the window. The sink was sited at the rear with water pumped by electricity from the 9gal (41ltr) underfloor tank. The stainless steel cooker/grill was housed in a cabinet by the sliding door and cooking or washing could be done in comfort either standing or sitting. A wardrobe unit was sited in the rear opposite the spare wheel.

Cabinet work was in light oak scratch-resistant laminate and the food cupboard was lined in laminate for complete hygiene. Orange curtaining and oatmeal check upholstery were typical for the time. The 'room for loving' theme was developed by a racy (for then) picture of a couple in bed in the 'Boudoir' area listening to the 'stereo system for mood music and a radio to keep in touch with civilisation'! The Philips stereo cassette system was standard and Viking was the first converter to offer a sound system as standard equipment.

As well as the optional pop-top roof, a front roof rack and cab hammock bunk were available as extras, as was the 'Isabella Awning'. This free-standing tent could sleep three in comfort and was the very latest in frame tent design. Also optional were the 1700cc engine, automatic transmission and a heated rear window.

Interestingly, the new Viking precipitated a major row between Volkswagen GB and the motorhome industry. In 1972 VW GB had entered into an exclusive contract with Devon, meaning that only Devon conversions were now officially VW-approved (apart from Westfalia). VW GB claimed other conversions that involved cutting the roof were unsafe because they lacked extra underfloor and roof strengthening and withdrew its warranty on any such vehicle. In a press release headed, 'VW Warning on Unauthorized Motor Caravans', VW GB cited the Viking conversion as a prime example. Motorhomes hit back, challenging VW to carry out a thorough technical appraisal, claiming, 'their concern for safety is nothing but a device which they are exploiting in an effort to discredit what most observers consider to be the best conversion ever built on a VW chassis, the Viking Motorhome.' The motoring press of the time tended to agree with the general view that the VW marketing policy played a major role in the controversy!

Despite the claims from VW GB, Viking went on to produce what was to become one of the most spacious and sought-after elevating roofs, and no records show that Viking, or any of

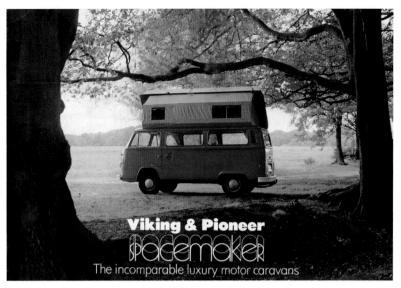

The Spacemaker roof was launched in 1974.

the other professional conversions, was structurally unsound or unsafe! Viking advertising from 1973 fought back stating:

> The Viking invaders have arrived. The biggest battle in motor caravan history has begun. It will be hard. It will be long. And you are a witness. Viking Motorhomes on one side; Devon and Westfalia on the other. David and Goliath all over again. You were born to be free. You buy a motor caravan to stay free. Your freedom gives you the right to choose. Before you buy, insist on seeing a Viking. We'll send a Viking to your door. If you're sure it's what you want we'll build one just for you. One more Viking on our side. One more blow for freedom.

THE VIKING AND PIONEER SPACEMAKER

By 1973 Motorhomes had become Motorhomes International and had relocated to Stanbridge in Bedfordshire. In 1974 a brand new Viking conversion was launched, with the now much sought-after large roof, designated the Viking Spacemaker.

The innovative, new Viking Roof was also promoted as an aftermarket roof, meaning that customers could have one fitted to their existing motor caravan, by Motorhomes or any garage. This explains why some other conversions like Devons are found with Viking roofs fitted.

The roof was the big selling point – no other conversion offered such space – three wide sleeping areas

made up of a 6ft (1.8m) bunk running down each side, and another running across the width at the front, formed a U shape. The roof was side hinged, with a tent extension along the loading door side, into which one berth flapped out (instead of in) to form the base. The roof had two windows and two air vents and the fitting of gas struts as standard made lifting the extra weight much easier.

The interior layout was redesigned; it was still different from the common arrangements, and reminiscent of the 1960s Dormobiles in that the two-burner cooker and grill was sited centrally in a unit across the rear section, allowing cooking centrally inside the vehicle either seated or standing up. A small front section flapped open to access the grill. The cooker was flanked on each side with storage cupboards with worktops, with a roof locker above. On later units, fitted with mains hook-up, a Zig control panel was sited on the left of this.

The stainless steel sink and drainer were housed on the loading door side, with a small side cupboard under. A

The huge roof with ample sleeping space was a Viking innovation and a key selling point.

For travelling all seats could face forwards.

The kitchen layout at the rear stayed the same, but cabinets were now finished in dark veneer.

The Pioneer was the budget model, without a fitted kitchen.

gas or electric fridge, with cutlery drawer over it for later units, was sited at the end of the unit with its door accessed by the sliding door. One of the other main selling points of the Viking was the large capacity water tank – 10gal (45.5ltr) could be carried in the tank, which was slung under the floor. This feature was actually used by Holdsworth (*see* Chapter 17) to promote their own conversion, in an aggressive advertising campaign that focused on how some features were not quite as good as they claimed to be, in this case highlighting the difficulty of cleaning such a tank and the wind resistance from the large roof!

The section between the rear seat and sink unit, which accessed the cooker, could be used as a rear bench seat by using a removable board. At the rear were twin curtained wardrobes. The front seats could be arranged to face forwards for travelling, or dinette style to face the rear bench to seat four in comfort around the table. Fluorescent lights were fitted above both sections of the side window, with two louvred side windows also fitted as standard.

The interior was well appointed and colour co-ordinated. Earlier models had plain leatherette upholstery and trim, but on the later ones the cushioning was reversible with one side and the edges being wipe-clean leatherette (commonly brown), with brown/white/oatmeal check cloth on the reverse. The cab seats were finished in matching leatherette, with check fabric seat and back for later models.

Later models also featured padded leatherette panelling on walls and the sliding door, which was topped under the side windows with matching check fabric. Inset under the window side were two deep storage pockets, faced with the same check upholstery

fabric. The bunk edges were also faced with padded leatherette. Cabinet work was in medium wood grain laminate. The table top was matching wood laminate and a fitted beige carpet added to the co-ordinated interior.

Tables were stored under the two rear facing single seats, and a buddy centre seat was available for the middle. The seating laid down to form a bed of legendary proportions, which covered the whole load area almost right up to the sliding door.

Also available from 1974 was a basic version designated the Viking Pioneer. Advertised as 'a simple, unsophisticated motor caravan built to a standard of excellence to match the worthy Volkswagen', the pioneer also featured eight forward-facing seats that could be arranged dinette style round a table or laid down to form two single beds or a king-size double. Above the engine was a mattress to give sleeping space for two small children and a cab hammock bunk could be specified for additional sleeping space. The Spacemaker roof could also be fitted as an option. Sited behind the front passenger seat, by the sliding door, was a camping style twin-burner cooker and grill. No water or washing facilities were provided apart from a plastic bowl and water bottles.

Viking Motorhomes would also convert a used vehicle claiming, 'Once we've finished with the interior it will be almost indistinguishable from a new van costing perhaps £1,000 more. We'll carry out all the work to the same perfection as our new models.' Furthermore, the interior fittings were also available in kit form for DIY assembly. The dealership would arrange for the vehicle to have the windows and roof fitted by Viking, who would then provide side wall panels, flooring kit, cushions, curtains,

curtain rail, cooker and so on with all units ready assembled for fitting. The only optional extra for the kit version was the fridge. Back in 1974, fitting out your Camper yourself, using the Viking kit, saved around £400 on the conversion charge.

The Viking featured here is a 1979 model, called the Spacemaker Six. It is completely original inside, even down to the carpet and curtains, and the photographs show the interior colours, layout and the large sleeping space clearly. Owned by Von and Shaun the Bus was originally bought from Land Carriage, a firm that dealt solely with VW Campers. The Viking conversion was used on the front cover of their brochure and was profiled first in their model details. They sold new and used VW Campers including Vikings, Devons, Danburys, Dormobiles and Westfalias, and they would also fit any of those conversions to a used vehicle on request. A customer could even hire a Camper for a holiday to test out, and if they subsequently bought it, the hire price was refunded! As well as Camper hire they also ran a buy-back scheme for overseas visitors.

The Viking conversion continued to be offered on the T25 range, featuring a very similar layout, but stiff competition and dwindling sales forced Viking to cease operation by the mid-1980s.

Windows and roofs could be fitted to private vehicles in the Viking workshops.

The bulkhead seating can be as two singles or a bench by using a buddy seat in the gangway.

The sink is sited at one side, with the cooker over the rear deck.

1979 Viking Spacemaker Six.

The increased space is achieved by having the roof 'overhang' along one side.

The lower berth is a roomy and comfortable double bed.

Alternatively, the whole interior can lay out right up to the door, creating even more sleeping space.

The deep, reversible cushions, with check fabric on one side, are all original. Mounts for the table can be seen on the padded side panel.

Storage pocket fronts are finished in a matching fabric, and trimming is right up to the windows. The interior panels are clad with padded vinyl.

The sliding door is also clad in padded vinyl.

The roof has three/four bunks, trimmed to match the interior and cab seats.

The Zig control panel can be seen bottom left.

Bulli-Kartei at the Westfalia Werks.

LEADING THE WAY

Westfalia Werks was founded by Johann Knobel in October 1844 as a blacksmiths and agricultural tool factory. This extended into harnesses and then horse-drawn carts; eventually a special paint and upholstery section was created to cater for a new range of more luxurious, high-quality carriages for people transport. At the end of the 1920s Westfalia began to produce caravans and multi-purpose trailers, and by the late 1930s were also producing camping trailers including the now highly sought-after teardrop trailers. Despite enormous damage during World War II, the factory managed to restart production and in 1948 exhibited a steel-plated caravan at the Hanover Motor Fair.

In the late 1940s and early 1950s people simply could not afford a second vehicle; they therefore required a vehicle to be both a weekday workhorse and a weekend wanderer. Hence the particular success of the Kombi! In the same way that the folk at Dormobile, also in 1951, drew inspiration from seeing people sleeping in cars at Dover, Westfalia soon saw how the Kombi was proving successful at meeting both work and leisure needs. In 1951 they were approached by a US officer, posted in Germany, to build an interior for a VW Transporter, styled on

caravan designs. After this one-off order, Westfalia Werks went on to hand build individually approximately fifty more (*see* 'The First Full Camping Interior' below); these prototypes were to become the basis for the models produced in 1955. In 1953 Westfalia introduced the Camping Box – a set of furniture that could be quickly installed and removed which would transform the weekday workhorse into a hotel on wheels. From 1955 a full camping interior was available and by 1957 Westfalia had produced its one-thousandth Camper

conversion. Up until 1958 Westfalia would convert Buses for private individuals who brought their Buses to the factory; thereafter this was for special (and rich) customers only!

By the early 1970s the assembly line had a continuous production line of thirty-eight vehicles with a capacity of 135 daily. The factory was turning out 30,000 units annually, with 75 per cent of these going to America. Using VW factory sunroof models, already strengthened for the sunroof but minus the gear, it took approximately two hours for a vehicle to be fully fitted out, including the fitting of the elevating roof. Impressive!

The relationship between VW and Westfalia thrived through succeeding generations of Transporter, but finished in 2004 when VW decided to produce its own camping conversion on the new T5 base. The reason for this was quite simple – Westfalia were by now owned by Daimler/Chrysler/Mercedes-Benz. Previously, Volkswagen had always given Westfalia one of its new generation prototypes and Westfalia had been able to suggest changes before full-scale production commenced; however, VW saw no reason to give a company, now owned by a major competitor, sight of its new T5 platform and so opted to produce its own Camper, ending a partnership that spanned fifty-three years.

On parade : new 1958 US export models.

1951: THE FIRST FULL CAMPING INTERIOR

Around fifty fitted-out Campers were produced in 1951–52, one of which was exhibited at the 1952 Frankfurt Motor Show. Pictured here is one of those 1952 Kombi models, AB 877-444, with a fitted Westfalia Camping interior; it was also one of the first of the prototype Campers to have the new roof hatch. The interior was not Camping Box, but consisted of fixed, boxed units, including a tall side cupboard sited by the rear loading door that was to become the wardrobe in future Westfalia Campers. The Bus was also finished in a distinctive colour scheme of tan and yellow, and had the brown/yellow/beige check curtains and birch ply panels/headlining that were to become other distinctive Westfalia features. Erna and Helmut Blenck bought the Camper in 1952 and spent 1953 travelling across Southern Africa. Their book about their epic travels, *South Africa Today*, was published in 1954. The photo of them crossing a dry river bed on the edge of the Kalahari Desert shows the tin hatch in front of the roof rack, which has been mounted onto the roof and secured with screws from inside the van.

The original interior (or purportedly some of it) fitted in this Camper currently resides in the Westfalia museum.

1953: THE FIRST CAMPING BOX

Applying expertise gained from building caravans and camping trailers, in 1953 Westfalia produced the first production line camping equipment designed for the VW Camper. Known simply as the Camping Box, it was basically a self-contained unit that fitted against the front bulkhead, with bench seating, a unit for the loading door and a large cupboard in the rear.

The top of the main bulkhead unit was in three sections. In the middle a lid hinged up to reveal a two-burner cooker, and a drawer flanked this on either side with additional storage under the lid of the section by the

This 1952 fully fitted Westfalia Camper travelled across Africa in 1953. The red pin-striping can just be seen round the swage line.

Ihr Landhaus auf Rädern!

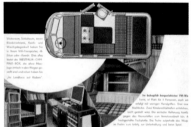

The first Camping Box brochure was produced in 1953. As well as showing layouts and optional tents, the brochure also showed how the unit could double up for guests in the house!

This early interior dates from 1954/55.

windows. On the loading door end of the unit was a rail for towels and tea cloths. The cushions were carried in the middle section of the unit, which was open and fronted by a fold-up removable door in the centre that doubled as table or bed support. Upholstery was in the distinctive check plaid fabric that was to become a feature of Westy interiors right through the generations. The bottom of the unit had three separate flap-up storage compartments. Seating was a metal-framed rear bench and smaller seat section under the side windows, which laid flat to form a double bed. Affixed to the rear loading door was a toiletry unit that comprised shelved storage with a flap-down shelf at the bottom to hold an enamel washing bowl and a flap-up vanity mirror at the top. Above the engine compartment was a large clothes/linen cupboard, which nearly filled the entire space. This had sliding doors and a central shelf. All units were finished in medium finish grained wood.

Hardly anything fully original survives from this period; for example, there are no known vehicles with an original large rear cupboard unit still fitted. It is possible that the brochures of the time depicted kitted-out prototypes featuring all the units, whereas in reality most customers simply opted for the bulkhead unit and seating; conversely it may simply be that some units and fittings, which were in place, have not survived use over the years.

The distinctive Westy roof hatch (sometimes known as a 'submarine hatch') was introduced in 1952 and remained a standard part of Westfalia options till the unveiling of the new Westy pop-top roof in November 1964. This roof hatch could be fixed in various open positions and offered passengers the chance to admire the view whilst on the move, or gaze at the stars when asleep! From 1955 the roof hatch was a standard feature for all Export model Camping Box versions. From 1953 two sizes of sun canopy awning were also available, as was a full length roof rack.

1955: STANDARD AND EXPORT CAMPING BOXES

By 1955 Westfalia were producing two versions of the Camping Box, Standard and Export, offering two different systems to meet different markets.

The Standard

The Standard was similar in many ways to the previous Camping Boxes, and was usually supplied without the roof hatch conversion. Essentially it consisted of a large unit that fixed to the front bulkhead. A side-hinged lid at the loading door end revealed a single burner cooker, whilst the rest of the top was clear. A small drawer was fitted at the window end. The unit was open fronted with a flap-up table in the middle of the centre section where the bed cushions were carried. The bottom section was now open and housed the supporting boards along with two gas bottles, which were sited at the loading door end. Because the unit was completely free-standing and self-contained, literature of the time advertised the unit as ideal for putting up guests at home (when not in use in the Bus!).

It was also possible to turn the top of the unit into a child's berth, using the flap table in the vertical position to prevent rolling into the sleeping area and the brackets of the driver's backrest to prevent rolling into the cab. There was also an option to make an extra child's berth by swinging the cab bench seat back up to fit into a curtain pocket, though one wonders how much weight the arrangement would have supported!

A large three-section cupboard, now with roll-up doors, was sited above the engine, again filling almost the entire space. The large middle section was for clothes (and could hang jackets and the like), whilst the flanking side compartments were shelved. The washing and shaving cabinet for the loading door remained

The new Westfalia Camping Equipment was profiled in Popular Mechanics *in July 1955. Note the material pouch to support the seat back when turned into a child's bed.*

the same in appearance and design as for previous versions.

Curtains, mounted on rods, for the side windows were provided, along with a roof carrier and a large and small tent awning. Two types of tent awning continued to be available – the peaked roof version and the flat-topped tent, which was less expensive. Both had the same overall size, and were single room; just the roof was different. Roof racks could be full length racks with the mounts on the legs of the rack. Buses without racks had steel mounts fixed to the roof. Both Kombis and Microbuses had Camping Boxes installed and the factory paint scheme was usually retained (*see* below).

The Export

The Export model was a classier version of the Standard, and in many ways it was very similar to the 1952 Bus camping interior as described above, with all interior panelling and headlining in birch ply. Also standard was the roof hatch, a small sunshade awning and the famous Westy roof rack with polished aluminium bows and hardwood slats. Exports were also available finished in two-tone – not always using the standard VW colours of the time (*see* below).

Two steel-framed units provided seating at the rear and under the windows. The two bolsters of the side bench – one taken from its backrest – together with the auxiliary frame, which was simply pushed under the side bench, formed the bed. The rear bench unit now was enclosed to provide additional storage. A folding table was fitted centrally against the bulkhead, with a bulkhead flap seat next to it, by the loading doors. Curtains to all side windows were provided, along with curtaining between the front cab and living area. Also included were rubber mats for the load area floor and for the luggage area above the engine at the rear of the roller door cupboard.

No cooker or washing facilities were included, but the toiletry unit for the rear loading door (as fitted to the Standard) was available as an optional extra, as were awning sets with either a flat or peaked top.

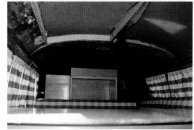

This 1955 Export Camping Box is one of the earliest known surviving examples. It is owned by Thom Fitzpatrick, who is painstakingly restoring it. The L-shaped seating, rear cupboard unit, toiletry cupboard and table arrangement can be seen, as can the wood panels and headlining.

The Westfalia tent could be used as a sun awning or tent.

1956: WESTFALIA DELUXE CAMPING EQUIPMENT

Introduced in 1956, The Deluxe Camping Equipment was heralded by Westfalia with:

Don't you sometimes long to leave life's hurly burly behind you and go out into the wide world and pause in woods and meadows, by inviting lakes and hills, to camp where the restraining arm of civilization cannot reach you? With the Westfalia Deluxe Camping Equipment you can transform your dreams into wonderful reality, giving you the chance of exploring nature's nooks and crannies, exchanging the bustle of the main road for the windings of a country lane … This holiday home on wheels will transform the world

into an exciting picture book for you where every page is a new and satisfying experience.

The specifications made this fantasy a reality – the Deluxe Camping Equipment was the first production line, fully kitted camping conversion, against which others would have to measure themselves. (Peter Pitt designed his interior for a VW Bus around the same time in the UK, but this did not go into full production until 1960; *see* Chapter 9.)

Fitted as standard were birch ply panelling to roof and side panels, a roof hatch, roof rack and large tent awning. Finished in light oak, the cabinet layout set the pattern for future Westies and VW Campers in

WESTFALIA
presents the holiday home on wheels

Volkswagen Kombi with Westfalia de Luxe Camping Equipment

Presented by:

Make more of your leisure and your holidays –
the VW Kombi with Westfalia de Luxe Camping Equipment
opens a whole new field of intriguing possibilities!
We should be glad to send you full particulars.
Just drop us a line.

Westfalia Werke KG · Wiedenbrück/Westf. [Germany] · Tel. 240

The manufacturer reserves the right to change illustrations and specifications. Printed in Germany.

general. Two enclosed bench seats, with storage under, were arranged dinette fashion around a flap-down table affixed to the side wall. The table dropped down between the benches to form the double bed. Between the front bench and the bulkhead was deep storage space for extra cushions, topped with a shelf unit. Just inside the front loading door was a unit that housed a single-burner gas cooker, complete with a heat-resistant, fold-up splash/wind guard. Under this was a cupboard space for pots and pans or the gas bottle. A wardrobe was fitted just inside the rear loading door. At the rear was a large 60ltr plastic-lined cool box fitted into a cabinet, with a crockery cupboard over. Behind this was space to carry two gas bottles or a fresh water container. A gas fridge was available as an option instead of the cool box. Opposite this, on the driver's side, were two further cupboards, the larger for clothes and the smaller for linen/bedding. These were centrally hinged so that access to clothes was from inside, whilst access to the other cupboard was via the rear hatch.

Curtains were fitted to all windows and also between the cab and living area. Upholstery and curtain material moved away from the familiar plaid checks to a modern, more abstract fabric design using Moltopren moth and termite proof material.

All of these early models used a set of very prominent decals with the Westfalia horse logo.

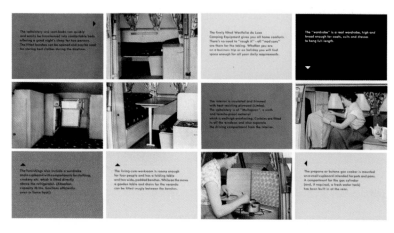

The Deluxe Camping Equipment, introduced in 1956, was the first fully fitted Camper with wardrobe, cooker and cool box. Note the curtains and cushion fabric designs, and Westfalia's own exterior paint colours.

1958–62
SO 22 CAMPING BOX AND MOSAIK
SO 23 CAMPINGWAGEN

In 1958 a revised version of the Camping Box was brought out, designated SO 22. Similar in design to the early Camping Boxes, it was essentially a self-contained unit with two metal-framed open bench seats and cushions stored in an open-fronted unit topped with three drawers. Under these was stored the table. The seats made up into a bed and allowed for the Kombi to serve as a load carrier during the week and as a weekend Camper for the family simply by the installation of the unit against the front bulkhead – something Westfalia (and others) were keen to promote! Optional equipment included a two-burner petrol cooker and some cupboard units.

In 1960 the Camping Box became the Camping Mosaik, still carrying the designation SO 22. The Mosaik version, however, allowed you to buy all the parts for a camping conversion in kit form, either piece by piece or just the pieces you needed for your own requirements. The new kit consisted of two bench units, a table, toiletry cupboard for the loading door, a wardrobe, rear side cupboard with two doors and a child's cab hammock. This design was revamped in 1962 and sold fully installed (as SO 33), or the new Camping Mosaik (SO 22).

In late 1958 the Deluxe Camping Equipment was revised again, and marketed in the USA as the Westfalia Deluxe Camping Equipment 59. In fact, this interior was almost identical to the interior layout that became the SO 23.

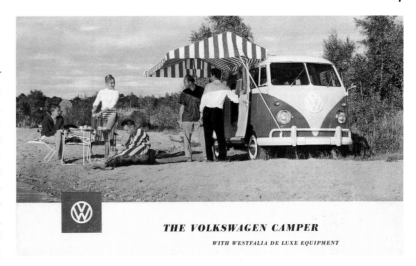

THE VOLKSWAGEN CAMPER

WITH WESTFALIA DE LUXE EQUIPMENT

THE VOLKSWAGEN CAMPER

WITH WESTFALIA DE LUXE EQUIPMENT

1958/59 Deluxe Camping Equipment brochures.

A refurbished 1957 Deluxe interior. Note the prominent Westfalia decal.

The cooker was standard equipment with this model.

This 1956 Westfalia is owned by Jim Phillips who has restored its original and rare tan and yellow colour scheme. He has also fitted a 1958 Camping Box. Period accessories, such as the camping chairs, help to recreate the look. The upholstery has been replaced, but all the fitments are original 1958 equipment. Note the silver Temprite cool box on the rear deck – a 1950s US period accessory.

SO 23

Available from 1959, the SO 23 was a very different affair and set the standard in design and fittings that became the hallmark of Westfalia Campers. The SO designation, shortened from Sonderausführungen (sonder = special) was now officially adopted for special body conversions or fitments, and applied to commercials as well as Westfalia Campers. There was still a Standard and Deluxe version – the Deluxe included the rear cool box unit. Cabinet work was finished in wood finish plywood veneer and the doors were oval or half rounds in shape with metal edging. Upholstery was in red and black, or yellow and black check plaid, with matching curtains (red for red/black

and yellow for yellow/black seats), and the seating was arranged round the table, with the two back cushions laying out on the dropped table position to form the bed. An early style child's hammock hooked around the back of the front seat to make a small hammock bunk, with the bottom of the seat as the lower berth. A toiletry/washing unit was sited to the left of the loading doors behind the passenger. An electric siphon hose fed water from a large tank (20gal (90ltr)) stored under the seat behind the driver. The front of the unit was a shelved cupboard for storing the bowl and kitchen utensils. On the side of this unit was a flap-down shelf to hold a washing bowl.

Fixed to the top and rear of this unit was the first 'cocktail cabinet',

which consisted of a spun coloured aluminium drinks set comprising 6oz cups and shot glasses housed under a clear perspex box lid. Another touch of class was added with the fitting of two clamshell design side lights opposite the loading doors.

A wardrobe with dressing mirror was sited just inside the rear loading door. An optional cool box section (which had been standard on the slightly earlier Deluxe), which included another storage compartment, was sited on the driver's side above the engine compartment. Fitted as standard was a cargo net for shoes across the ceiling of the rear area, a large one for the Standard version and a smaller one for the Deluxe version.

Sisal carpet flooring was fitted in the load area and attached in place with press studs; the rear deck above the engine was covered with brown or green linoleum commonly known as marble mat because of the marbled pattern effect.

The tent awning was the large swing-out style in red and white stripe. This was held in place with special mounts on the roof and front bumper, and with a drilling in the rear bumper. Also now available was the new style Westfalia roof rack, which sat a little higher than previous versions. Earlier racks are identifiable from the side profile – the back bow has a lower profile, whereas later racks all had equal bow height. The attaching clamps are smaller without press marks from stamping. Also the wood slats were screwed with two screws, instead of one as in later racks. The very early racks can be distinguished by legs that were square tubing – 1957–58 racks had the inverted U-shaped tubing, whereas from 1959 onwards the inverted U shape was pressed from flat steel.

Kombis were the base model for all SO 23s and many were factory fitted, with the options of six pop-out side windows and front-opening safari windows. Optional accessories included an Enders two-burner petrol cooker (model 9065D), a chemical toilet and the rear cool box unit.

The 1960 SO 23 featured overleaf is not only completely original, it also has a fascinating history.

Sisters Elva and Wilma Dittman lived together in Long Beach, California, and, with retirement approaching, were looking to get out on the road in a small, self-contained Camper and see the world. In 1959 they typed a carefully worded letter to the Westfalia factory enquiring about the company's new Volkswagen Camper conversions. A clerk at Westfaliawerk GmbH took the time to write back with detailed information about the sleeping arrangements and food storage, and included price sheets and factory descriptions (this correspondence is still with the Bus today).

As a result, they ordered a 1960 model year Westfalia Camper, with Deluxe interior, through their local VW dealer and made the necessary arrangements to pick up their Camper as a 'Tourist Delivery' in Germany. They travelled by train to New York and by ship to England and finally Hamburg, where they took delivery of their new Camper. They then travelled throughout Europe before shipping the Bus to NYC; the sisters then drove the Westy back to their home in Long Beach. Amazingly, the sisters duplicated this same trip in 1964, first driving back to NYC to travel by ship for their European tour. The 1960 Westfalia was the only car the sisters were to own for the rest of their lives, and was used as their grocery-getter as well as to escape from the city to go bird watching or to camp. Finally, in 1977, the Bus was pulled into their tiny one-car garage in the rear of their property for the last time, after logging 120,000 miles (193,080km) behind the wheel, as the sisters could no longer drive.

After Elva's death in 1996, nephew Jim came to live with Wilma to look after her and her dilapidated home. Jim knew that there was some old vehicle in the tumbledown garage and so hired a crew to demolish the garage carefully and remove the overgrowth to reveal the sisters' beloved Volkswagen covered in grime and sitting on four flat tyres. When he opened the cargo doors he was surprised to find that the entire original camping interior was in pristine condition. After having the local VW dealer perform basic mechanical work and a quickie detail job, Jim begin driving it around town for errands. On a whim, he drove it to a VW Jamboree in 1997, and that is when the second owner, Dave Kroesen, saw it for the first time. Jim and Dave became fast friends after Dave convinced him not to entertain selling it to the throngs of folks who were making offers left and right to buy it from him. Little did Dave know that six years later, and after buying and restoring several

early Westfalias, Jim would make the offer to sell it to him.

Once in Dave's care, the Bus received a full mechanical restoration. The motor, which was produced only two months after 'bastard' production stopped, still retained all of its post-bastard parts: smooth generator stand; 36hp sheet metal; early electric-choke carburettor; upward-discharge fuel pump; and thin-slot generator. Dave was surprised to find that the Bus still had its original axle boots and starter, and that it had never had an inside rear view mirror, seat belts or radio installed. Everything was removed from the underside and the inside of the Bus to reveal a bare can, which was cleaned and polished for reassembly. Dave even found camping receipts and European postcards dated 1960 throughout the cabinets. Jim told Dave that the sisters were small women, which has a lot to do with the minimal wear on the seat fabric, door panels and camping interior. Still today you can see the wear marks in the front seat upholstery where their wind-up phonograph rested as they bounced down the road!

As well as being in amazing condition, all the accessories are still intact, including the original canvas tent, poles, stakes and cord to produce the entire camping set-up, including the small potty-haus. The toilet bucket and seat are in well-preserved condition, as are the bar set, clamshell lights, wedge pillows, water storage tank and pump, wood slat roof rack, stove, sisal mat and rear cargo net. Also found within the Camper were two wooden deckchairs, used by the sisters on one of their transatlantic trips, with their names written on them, and shipping documents memorializing their world travel with their Camper.

After months of negotiations, Scott Doering finally acquired the Bus in March 2004, but subsequently sold it to Tony Best in the UK, who is now the proud owner of one of the most original condition early Westfalia Campers in the world.

This 1960 SO 23 is in immaculate original condition, even including the bucket toilet and seat, and has a fascinating history.

Without the sides the tent makes an excellent sun canopy.

The large tent awning has the optional toilet annexe. Note the ventilation holes!

Clamshell style lightshades add a stylish touch.

The original awning bag can be seen on the right.

The interior view is reminiscent of the original brochure shots.

The cocktail cabinet provides a classy touch.

Enamel bowls and syphon pump hose are stored in the side unit.

The 1961 SO 23 below is very special as it is the only walk-through version known to have been built, and was built to special order. The American who bought it flew to Germany, in April 1961, to buy a Westfalia direct from the Werks, and, on arrival, was picked up in a new SO 34 with a white interior. He said it reminded him of being in an ambulance and wanted the wooden interior, as in the SO 23. As he was about to undertake a dangerous trip through Eastern Europe into the Middle East and Palestine, he specifically wanted a walk-through model so that he could be self-contained within the Bus. Westfalia therefore collected a six pop-out window Bus from the VW factory to convert especially for him! The Bus is also unusual in that it has all-red seat covers and curtains, instead of the usual plaid; very few were made with this 1961-only feature. Being walk-through meant that the spare wheel had to be sited in the rear; to hide it Westfalia made a special screening curtain. After several years of fraught negotiations, Mark Merz finally acquired the Bus from the eighty-nine year old original owner in 2004, and found that it still had all its original equipment, including the washing bowl and plastic dishes and a rare optional roof rack cover, as well as all the original sales receipts.

The pump is sited at the end of the front bench seat.

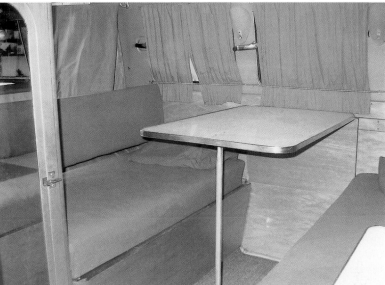

The all-red interior is an uncommon option, available only in 1961.

The cool box is sited in the rear. Note the marble mat over the rear deck.

The front bench means that the walk-through access is restricted, but possible.

The spare wheel has a matching cover.

A cargo net for shoes and the like was slung in the roof at the rear.

The original plastic washing bowl still carries the maker's decals.

A rarely seen option is the original Westfalia roof rack cover.

1961–65
SO 34 SO 35

In spring 1961, Westfalia Campers had another makeover, with the new versions being designated SO 34 and 35. SO 23 continued to be available until April 1961. The new models are often referred to as 'flip seat' models because of the unique front seat arrangement that allowed the back of the cab seat to flip through 180 degrees to form either dining seating or cab seating. The SO number referred to the upholstery and finish, with SO 34 being white and grey laminate and SO 35 finished in dark Swiss pear wood. The upholstery was either yellow/orange plaid Pendleton wool with a red vinyl front seat or blue/green plaid. The submarine roof hatch was still standard on both versions, but it now had a different prop rod that slid inside a channel on the hatch frame.

The Camper interior was now laid out as in the old style Export version, with seating under the windows opposite the loading doors, looking out of the side doors rather than facing each other front to back. The bed was made up from three narrow cushions going lengthwise in the middle of the Bus, using the front seat and the fold-up middle seat as extra space/length if needed. The front cab seat back, however, could flip back to provide rear-facing seating for dining/living, thus making the living area larger. A child's hammock could be fixed above the front cab seat using the flip seat in raised position for extra support.

The table had a Getalit top and screwed into the floor, but it could swivel on a vertical tube leg that allowed the long way to be either horizontal or vertical across the Bus, and it was possible to use the table

The SO 34 brochure images featured staged family camping scenes.

Is it a boat?

This distinctive SO 34 brochure took a more oblique approach.

This period photograph shows the unusual table mounted in the spare wheel set-up.

outside by fitting the leg into the spare wheel as a base. Three 2.2gal (10ltr) water containers were stored under the long bench seat, just behind the driver.

The wardrobe was sited in the same place by the rear loading door but was now wider, giving more space. Opposite that was the insulated cool box cabinet, at the front of which were two bar compartments, with racks and six 8oz coloured aluminium beakers. Between these was an adjustable two-position seat, which slid out into the living area, and folded down to double as a worktop. Under this was more storage space. A portable collapsible seat was sited just in front of the wardrobe.

At the rear was a two-door clothes and linen cupboard, opposite which was the swinging pantry cupboard. This could be swung out to be used

from the rear hatch or could swing to access from inside. An optional two-burner portable petrol cooker could be stored in the swing-out pantry unit, and could be used inside on the folded seat worktop. On the front loading door was a cabinet for washing and toiletries equipped with a wash bowl, mirror and two shelves.

The floor was sisal carpeting on top of plywood. There was also a socket for electric appliances and a cone-shaped detachable roof lamp that could be hung inside or outside, wherever needed. Also standard was a roof rack and mounting brackets for large and small optional tents. Other options included a portable chemical toilet, stationary heater and electric roof fans. From 1963 it was also possible to specify the Martin Walter elevating Dormobile roof to all Westfalia models.

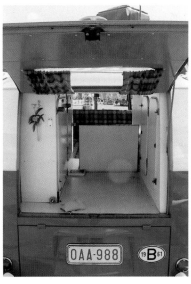

This Dutch SO 34 was seen at Bad Camberg 2003.

The wheel to enable the pantry unit to swing out is visible centre left.

The one-owner SO 34 featured here was built on 10 April 1964 as a Microbus and supplied with the then optional 1500cc engine. It was painted by Westfalia in Beige Grey (Light Grey, code 703). Bought on the 'grey' market in Europe, in 1964, it was shipped to the United States and sold to a German woman in Salem, Oregon, in late 1964. She owned it until 1998, when she became too old to drive, at which time Joe Crockett bought the Bus. It is in immaculate condition, with all the original equipment including the original upholstery throughout, complete with the 'wedge' pillows. The original Hunnersdorf water bottles are in place under the bed. It has both tents, the smaller Foyer tent, and the larger privy tent, in their original bags. It also has the original yellow lantern that plugs into the accessory socket above the side closet door, the optional folding metal chair in original upholstery and the wooden toilet. The Enders cooker and optional benzine filling cans are in the back pantry. Original fitted options include a locking steering column and Blaupunkt AM radio. Joe has added a Rosenthal vase and 100km badge and rebuilt the original transmission and motor. As this Westfalia model was not built for the US market, when it arrived in the US, the headlights were changed to sealed beam units (Joe has since changed them back to bulb type), and the speedometer was changed to a miles per hour unit.

This 1964 SO 34 is seen here with the small tent awning in grey and yellow.

The cocktail cabinet, with spun beakers, is sited on the rear unit, by the seats.

Seating is arranged under the window. Note the original lifter cushions and white cabinet work.

The cool box is complete with plastic bowl/storage.

A folding chair was provided for additional seating.

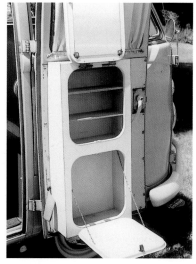

The toiletry cabinet has a flap-up mirror, which attaches to the door top with a plastic strap.

Behind the cool box is the swing-out pantry unit, here with optional original Enders cooker and fuel cans.

The spare wheel, complete with matching cover, is stored behind the pantry unit.

Three water bottles were stored under the bench seat.

The original Hünersdorff water bottles are complete and with the maker's decals.

A conical hanging light allowed for flexible lighting, inside or out.

The original wooden seat and toilet bucket.

SO 33 and Camping Mosaik 22

From 1962 another version was available in kit form. SO 33 was used to designate the permanently installed kit, whilst Mosaik 22 was the designation of the actual kit that could be bought in pieces. The kit was fully removable, allowing the Bus to be used for other purposes. With this system each item could be purchased separately, piece by piece. The literature of the time extolled the virtues of this approach with:

> Of course, this equipment is removable. It can be installed easily. And taken out easily. So you can make any VW Kombi or Microbus – old and new – into a camping car. Six days a week your VW assists you in earning money. It transports. It caters. It delivers and returns. On weekends it is your bungalow on wheels and helps you rest and relax wherever you please.

Interestingly, the 1963–64 kit was reminiscent of the earlier design with two bench seats opposite each other and the table in-between them. To make the bed, one seat bottom slid to the middle and the seat backs came off and were used to fill in the gaps. The front seat back was thinner and needed to use lifters to level out the bed. These were small, hinged pieces of wood stored inside the forward seat compartment. Under the seat bottoms were large storage areas. The cupboards had squarer doors with rounded corners trimmed in plastic, but instead of the brass swivel latches used previously Westfalia now fitted less sturdy plastic pull knobs.

The wardrobe was similar to that in the SO 34/35. At the rear was a clothes and linen cupboard with shelves, opposite which was a 2cu ft cool box. On the front loading door was the toiletry cabinet equipped with wash bowl, mirror and shelves, whilst the rear loading door had a flap-up small table. A pantry compartment was also available. The roof hatch, detachable roof lamp, roof rack and mountings for optional tent(s) were also standard and options were as for the SO 34/5.

The Camping Mosaik 22 allowed for each item to be ordered and installed separately once the Kombi's seats had been removed. It consisted of the same units as on the SO 33, with the roof hatch, tents, cooker and so on also available as options. Also optional was a rod with curtain between the front cab and the living area, but the electric socket was not available.

Kombis or Microbuses just fitted with the Martin Walter Dormobile elevating roof were designated SO 36.

1965–67
SO 42 SO 44

The changes in tastes, lifestyles and general increasing affluence were evident in the new interior styles for the 1965 models. One of the key features was the adoption of a sprung pull-out bed (similar in style to a Z-bed), which meant no more laying out tables and cushions!

The submarine style roof hatch was replaced by three options: a standard fixed roof; Westfalia's own new pop-top elevating roof with canvas sides and the full length Martin Walter Dormobile roof, all of which came with the full range of extras and option packages. Interestingly, official dealer catalogues show it was still possible (in theory) to order SO 33 and 34 through 1965 and 1966, alongside the SO 42 and 44 versions.

SO 42

SO 42 was aimed at the export market and sold especially well in the US, which seemed to have an insatiable demand for Westfalia Campers. The dinette arrangement was reintroduced with a table that folded flat against the side wall when not in use. The cushions were covered in easy-to-clean solid colour (commonly brown-gold) vinyl for the export market or the yellow/orange or green check plaid for home and European markets. All units were finished in wood-look Getalit. A larger cool box unit (with door shelves and racks) with a small cutlery drawer above was now sited inside the front loading door. Whilst there was no sink, a pump tap on the top of the unit fed water from a water tank housed in the unit. On the other loading door was an open-fronted storage unit for utensils, food,

VW Camping Car 33 and VW Camping Car Mosaic 22

A brochure shot showing all the pieces ready for fitting.

This 1962 SO 33 in Sealing Wax Red looks terrific.

The interior layout was dinette style.

The cool box and pantry.

Linen and clothes cupboards.

The cool box had ample capacity.

spices and so on. Two fold-up tables provided extra working space – one was hinged on the side of the cool box cabinet and the other fixed to the front loading door. The wardrobe now had a long mirror on its door inside and a new roof cupboard above the engine compartment was fitted. At the rear the clothes cabinet now opened upwards, rather than sideways as in the past.

Bulkhead models had a double bench seat behind the bulkhead, whilst walk-through versions had a small jump seat between the sink unit and the single seat. Between the driver and the rear passenger was a lidded map storage compartment. Non-walk-through versions also had another storage cupboard at the very rear on the driver's side. The side lights were covered with rectangular slide-out covers.

An option available from North American dealerships was a front-mounted spare wheel carrier, which afforded more living space inside.

This 1967 SO 42 is a walk-through model, with the pop-up roof option.

The inside is fully original and unmarked.

The open storage unit on the rear door was adopted by nearly all the US Westy-influenced conversions.

The cab boasts a series of period accessories: 6V plug-in coffee maker; windscreen suction spotlight; bud vase; and cab door shelf.

A useful storage pocket behind the single seat.

A combined cool box and water pump tap unit. No sink was fitted to these models.

The original equipment Coleman cooker and Coleman water container have hardly seen use.

The buddy seat sits in the gangway, but has legs and can be sited elsewhere or outside.

This 1967 SO 44 with optional Dormobile roof fitted is owned by Michael Steinke.

SO 44

SO 44 used a very different layout and was designed specifically for bulkhead models and mainly marketed in Europe. The wardrobe was sited against the rear bulkhead behind the driver and a unit ran across the remainder of the bulkhead to the loading doors (similar in some ways to the early Camping Box arrangement).

The unit was in three sections – the one nearest the wardrobe had three shelves and plenty of storage for canned and dry goods. The middle one had three small utensil drawers and storage for the bottles whilst the compartment nearest the load doors held the cool box with two drawers above it. For 1967 an additional optional box unit could be sited on the top, which hinged up to reveal space for the (optional) cooker and a sink unit. Initially, water was obtained by siphon pumping from two removable bottles, but later models had a water tank installed. Flap-up tables were fitted to both loading doors.

The table was on a movable swivel and there was an additional seat under the windows between the wardrobe and rear bench seat. The bed was the same design as that in SO 42, using a simple action to pull out a fully sprung large double bed, which went from wall to wall. Upholstery was in plain yellow or plain red for Export models, or the yellow/orange or green plaid on European versions. Three large roof lockers were mounted above the engine compartment, giving plenty of storage but at the price of restricted view through the rear window.

The kitchen unit with sink and tap runs across the front bulkhead, with a wardrobe at the far end.

Camping Mosaik SO 45

This was the designation for the Camping Mosaik kit designed to fit any bulkhead model and used furniture and equipment as for SO 42, with all items available to purchase separately. It was available for 1967 only. All the furniture was finished in real wood veneer.

Three large roof lockers were mounted at the rear.

INTERIOR FITTINGS CODES

As well as customers being able to specify individual options, Westfalia also offered option packages, which combined a range of popular options, fittings and equipment. They were prefixed by a letter code.

SO 23 packages included:

A23: standard SO 23 Camper

B23: as A23 but with chemical toilet

D23: as B23 but with Enders petrol cooker and rear cool box unit.

For SO 33 the equipment options were:

A33: standard camping equipment with large tent awning

B33: as A33 plus chemical toilet and two-burner petrol cooker

D33: as A33 but with small tent awning

E33: as D33 but with chemical toilet and two-burner cooker.

SO 42 codes referred to the fitting (or not) of the new pop-top roof and were:

A42: standard SO 42 equipment and interior

B42: standard SO 42 with pop-top roof, side awning and roof rack

C42: standard SO 42 with pop-top roof only

D42: standard SO 42 with side awning and roof rack.

SO 36 was used to designate the Martin Walter elevating roof.

Camping equipment was also available packaged, especially for the Mosaik kits. Typical packages were:

F22: standard camping interior (seats and table), living and sleeping areas with separate curtaining, cushions and carpets

G22: as F22 but with wardrobe, sink, 55ltr cool box, children's hammock bed and washbasin

H22: as G22 but with small tent awning, roof bunks, folding table for side door

K22: as G22 with large tent awning, roof bunks, folding table for side door, chemical toilet, hanging light and cable, plug and socket, three 10ltr water containers and washing bowl.

WESTFALIA COLOURS

There are examples in the US of early Buses that were delivered in primer and painted at the factory, where they did not remove tail lights, door handles or window seals before they painted the Buses, and the original factory primer can still be found under these items if they are removed!

Until 1958, in addition to the VW colours, Westfalia also used some colour schemes of its own, such as yellow and tan as used on the 1952 Camper.

There are records of three-tone schemes (of yellow/tan/yellow and white/tan/white combinations, with the roof matching the lower body colour. These all had red pin-striping around the swage line). For 1957/58 a distinctive combination was grey blue/dark blue/grey blue, although the Palm Green over Sand Green is the most commonly seen colour on surviving examples. The dash top and shelf were often painted to match the exterior central body colour, as can be seen in the 1958 example below, which also features original pin-striping.

Interestingly, no records are available to document use of the colour schemes of yellow/black and red/black as seen on the early examples in the Westfalia Museum – if they are authentic they must have been to special order. It should be noted that the museum examples are not offered as originals, and, as in the Wolfsburg Museum, examples are not always what they may at first seem or purport to be!

From 1959 Westfalia used the standard single colour or two-tone combinations that were current VW colours, although previous years' colours were available to special order. Prior to that, Dove Blue, Pale Grey and Brown Beige over Light Beige were the most common colours. Some early Dove Blue versions had white pin-striping applied around the swage line.

BAY WINDOW WESTFALIAS: 1968–79

1968: SO 60/61/62

The new shape Westfalia Campers were available from January 1968 with the designations SO 60, 61 and 62. The old pop-top roof was replaced by a new style of elevating roof, hinged at the front and lifting in the middle to give maximum headroom in the living area. The rear section of the roof was a moulded built-in roof rack with integral struts, which could be accessed via a flap in the rear of the lifting roof. A new style of tent awning was also introduced, with the canvas hanging inside the metal frame. The pop-up top and metal roof rack options were still available. Built mainly on Kombi bases, paint colours were usually single colour, with the pop-top or elevating roof providing white contrast.

SO 60/61

SO 60 was the walk-through cab, more basic version with a single seat behind the driver (or passenger if RHD), and a water supply/sink unit opposite by the front of the sliding door. This unit had the water tank and a cool box under the sink and featured an open shelved storage unit with flap-up table/worktop fixed on the side facing out. The main table folded flat against the wall when not in use. The bench seat pulled out to form the bed and a wardrobe was sited just inside the sliding door.

SO 61 was the Camping Mosaik version of the above equipment.

SO 62

SO 62 was the fully equipped Camper, and the layout was closely modelled on the prior SO 44 Split Screen version. Behind the driver was the wardrobe and running across the rest of the front bulkhead was a large kitchen unit as fitted in SO 44. This featured a central drawer and three cupboards. The centre one was the large cool box. On top of this was another unit which ran two-thirds of the way across, with a lifting lid and the sides providing splash back

A 1968 SO 60 with new style front-hinged elevating roof option.

A 1968 SO 62 with pop-top roof option.

protection. The sink was sited in this at the left by the wardrobe, and the two-burner stainless steel cooker was next to it, in the middle above the drawer and cool box.

Above the flap down table was a reading light. At the rear above the engine compartment was a three section roof cabinet as used in SO 44.

1969–71: SO 69

For 1969 Westfalia expanded the range of models to cover various fixture permutations for several basic layouts. Each SO was given a model name after a major European city, thus:

SO 69/1 – 'Oslo'
SO 69/2 – 'Zurich'
SO 69/3 – 'Stockholm'
SO 69/4 – 'Brussels'
SO 69/5 – 'Paris'
SO 69/6 – 'Rome'
SO 69/7 – 'Amsterdam'.

The Oslo and Zurich models were virtually the same as SO 62, except that they now featured a swivelling table with a single seat base under the window. The Oslo was a bulkhead model with single and double cab seats, whilst the Zurich was a walk-through with two single cab seats and the spare wheel mounted at the rear at one side of the above-engine compartment.

The Stockholm and Brussels models were very similar but slightly more

Three styles of elevating roof were offered from 1969.

expensive, as they had an extra wardrobe and side rear linen cupboard (meaning that the bed was not full width), with the Stockholm being the single/double cab seat version. Neither of these had the roof cupboard.

The Paris and Rome were slightly cheaper versions. Both were the two single front seat walk-through models, but a cooker was not standard. A wardrobe was sited behind the driver with a sink/cool box unit opposite by the sliding door. This had an open shelved cupboard with flap table on the side by the door, and another flap-up seat/table on the gangway side. The Paris featured the full width bench seat/bed and roof cabinet, whilst the Rome had a further wardrobe plus rear linen cupboard on the sliding door side.

The Amsterdam was the walk-through budget model; instead of a wardrobe there was a single seat behind the driver, and the table flapped down against the side wall instead of being multi-position swivel.

This 1969 model follows the Amsterdam layout with flap-down table and single seat, though the cool box unit is missing.

On the sliding door side was a wardrobe and rear linen cupboard and the sink/cool box unit with side cupboard and a small flap-down table on each side. An upholstered stool could sit in the walk-through section or be moved to the area by the sliding door for day use.

New style Mosaik Kits appeared for 1970, designated SO 70 and SO 71. These were quite basic affairs consisting of rear bench seat, flap-down table, single seat behind the driver, and an upholstered stool. SO 71 was the full width rear seat/bed version and SO 70 the three-quarter width version (although it was still possible to buy the sink unit, wardrobe and other items from the previous Mosaik kits!).

All were based on Kombis and the Martin Walter full length elevating roof was still also available, in addition to the front-hinged and pop-top versions.

This particular model, owned by Johnathon and Nicky Crump, rolled off the production line in April 1969 with the layout known as SO 69/3, the Stockholm, and was fitted with an array of interesting options. M517 designated it as a Westfalia Campmobile with M518 for the raising roof. No code for the Dormobile roof exists, but M191 (the underfloor and belly strengthening plates) was used for Buses that would have large holes cut in the roof! Other options included Eberspächer heater, bulkhead model (Kombis and Microbuses were now commonly walk-through models), automatic side step, Emden radio, heated rear window and, unusually, M100 – no front VW badge! Finally, a 'packaged' option also saw the Bus fitted with ambulance fans, cargo net, tow hooks (front and back) and reversing lights.

This 1969 Westfalia Stockholm was ordered with the Dormobile roof option, side step and no front badge.

The wardrobe and pull-out bed.

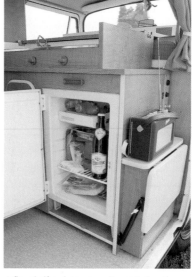

A flap shelf and storage unit are sited on the end of the kitchenette unit.

Cab bunks.

The kitchen is arranged across the bulkhead …

… with another wardrobe at the far end.

The kitchenette has plenty of storage plus a stainless steel cooker and sink/drainer, and a large cool box.

A cargo net is fitted in the rear of the roof.

1970: THE US CAMPMOBILE

VWoA introduced a US-only version this year, simply known as the VW Camper. Whether or not Westfalia actually made the fittings or licensed their manufacture is unclear, but the interior was almost the same layout as for the Amsterdam, except without an upholstered stool or gangway flap table. The furniture on some units was in light oak, not veneer, and the cupboard doors were rectangular with straight wood trim instead of the usual rounded plastic trimmed doors. There was, however, a roof storage shelf above the rear compartment. The spare tyre was mounted on the front and the Westfalia hanging tent awning and child cab hammock were

standard. The pop-top roof with metal roof rack was offered as an option, and instead of the front-hinged elevating roof option VWoA offered an elevating roof, manufactured by Sportsmobile, called the Penthouse Roof. This version, unlike that fitted to Sportsmobile Campers, was in two sections, like the normal Westy version but with the front above-cab section being the integral roof rack part. The whole of the middle/rear section raised vertically like a pop-top.

The early VWoA Campmobiles were based on Panel Vans and were converted in America using a Westfalia style and design of interior. The Sportsmobile Penthouse elevating roof was a new option, but the tent was a Westfalia model.

The lid of the unit flaps over into the cab for a large work surface.

VOLKSWAGEN CAMPER NEWS!

The factory-fitted tow hitch and reversing light.

1972: SO 72

In August 1972 the restyled Transporter with high front indicators was introduced and the front-hinged elevating roof option continued across both versions. However, from late 1973, the roof was hinged from the rear, with the roof rack space now over the front cab.

The new models were again named after cities, but now three models were specifically tailored to the US market and carried US city names:

SO 72/1 – 'Luxembourg'
SO 72/2 – 'Los Angeles'
SO 72/3 – 'Helsinki'
SO 72/4 – 'Houston'
SO 72/5 – 'Madrid'
SO 74/6 – 'Miami'.

The Helsinki was the top of the range option, the layout of which was almost the same as the earlier Paris, being a walk-through with wardrobe and sink/cool box unit sited on either side of the gangway against the front seats, full width rear seat/bed, under-window seat/storage, swivel table and roof cupboard, and spare wheel in the rear. However, a new style two-burner cooker unit was now sited against the wardrobe, which flapped down across the gangway and secured against the sink unit for use.

The US versions were known generically, and marketed as the Campmobile (in the same way as the Continental in the UK), rather than as Westfalias. In fact, many buyers probably thought they were buying a Camper built and assembled by VW! The Miami had the single seat and the sink/cool box unit with flap tables on both sides, the fold-down table on the sidewall, a wardrobe and rear linen cupboard on the sliding door side and three-quarter width rear bench seat/bed. It also featured the uphol-stered stool for extra seating. The Houston had the wardrobe behind the driver arrangement instead of the single seat, a swivel table and a roof cabinet and had the full width rear seat/bed. The Los Angeles had the extra side wardrobe and linen cup-boards, three-quarter seat/bed layout.

The Volkswagen Continental

1972: THE CONTINENTAL – AN RHD CONVERSION

The Continental was the name under which Westfalia Campers were mar-keted by VW GB. Its layout was almost identical to the Helsinki layout described above, with the wardrobe and cooker/sink across the front section, except that it was configured for RHD. It came with the elevating roof, cab hammock bunk and tent awning as standard. A refrigerator instead of the cool box was optional and the spare wheel had a vinyl cover. A free-standing upholstered stool was also standard with the Continental.

Walls and roof for all models were finished in wood grain birch ply. Upholstery was in Autumn Gold with white/brown/orange check curtains. Table surfaces were white, all work surfaces were in scratch-resistant laminated plastic and cabinet work was in the usual teak veneer with brown plastic door edge trim. Two louvred windows, with removable flyscreens, were fitted in the sliding door and opposite side window.

The 1972 example shown here is owned by Dave and Clare Simpkin. It features the Continental layout with the early style of front-hinged elevating roof.

Westy tent awnings of this period hung inside the frame and featured a striped sun canopy extension.

A free-standing stool was standard with the Continental.

The cool box door has not been rehung for the RHD configuration (probably too expensive to do), making access from outside more tricky.

The interior has been tastefully re-covered using a modern interpretation of the Westy plaid, colour matched to the vehicle.

The wardrobe is sited behind the driver and its door has been rehinged for the RHD configuration. The cooker is stored in the top flap-down door on the wardrobe side.

The cooker flaps down across the gangway for use and secures on the cool box/sink unit.

The large double pull-out bed uses the rear deck area and is full width.

The rear section of the roof had an integral roof rack, which could be accessed via the elevating roof canvas end panel.

1973–74: SO 73

The Frankfurt Motor Show in September 1973 saw the official unveiling of the new style of elevating roof that was hinged at the rear. The 1974 models on show featured yet another variant on the interior arrangements   with a sink unit now behind the driver and a cooker/cool box unit on the other side of the gangway by the sliding door. All models now came with the upholstered stool, and the European models still carried city names:

SO 73/1 Dusseldorf
SO 73/3 Malaga
SO 73/5 Offenbach.

The Dusseldorf had a sink unit with electric pumped water now sited behind the driver, with a water tank underneath. An upholstered stool could sit in the gangway or by the sliding doors. A new cooker unit now stood by the sliding door, with the two-burner gas cooker, a drawer underneath and the gas bottle in a cupboard under that. A flap-down table mounted on a small storage unit was fixed facing the outside. The rest of the layout was much the same as before, with swivel table, under window seat/storage, full width bench seat/bed, but the wardrobe was now sited on the rear driver s side wall and the closed roof cupboard was shorter to take account of this.

The Malaga had no rear wardrobe unit but had a vanity mirror by the sink unit and a full width roof cupboard, whilst the Offenbach had both the wardrobe and vanity mirror units! The visible spare wheel in the Malaga version was covered in the same plaid colour cloth as the seats.

Camping Mosaik versions were designated SO 73/7 and SO 78/8, depending on full width rear seat/bed, or three-quarter width unit plus side wardrobe and rear linen cupboard.

SO 73/2/4/6

The North American Export models were now referred to as Campmobile, and were offered in a similar range of combinations and alternative layouts as described for the European models,

1971 brochure shot

1973 brochure shot

One interesting US feature for the Campmobile was the collapsible spare wheel, stored under the sink unit, which came complete with a 12V compressor and electric cable.

but with some specific US market specifications and features such as mains and water hook-up.

The Campmobile

The standard Campmobile had the single seat and sink/cool box unit, upholstered stool, flap-down table, side wardrobe and rear linen cupboard arrangement. There was also an open-fronted roof cupboard, louvred windows on each side and a 12V reading lamp above the table. The table featured a special slide-out extension piece.

The Deluxe version came with an elevating roof (so no roof cupboard), and a gas cooker unit instead of the sink unit by the sliding door. Beneath the cooker was a refrigerator instead of a cool box. The propane gas tank was permanently mounted under the body beneath the sliding door, and was of the sort fitted to RVs. The sink unit was now sited behind the driver s seat and there was a clothes cabinet at the very rear on the same side. The closed upholstered stool doubled as a storage/trash container and the flap-down table had an extension piece. Also standard were an electric mains hook-up facility and connections (including hose) to the mains water supply for fresh water on site, plus a mosquito net screen for the rear hatch. Both versions included a tent awning and child s cab hammock bunk as standard.

1975–79: SO 76
THE BERLIN AND THE HELSINKI

1975 saw the introduction of two basic layouts   the Berlin and the Helsinki, designated SO 76/1 and 2 respectively, both available in fixed roof, pop-top roof or elevating roof versions. One new option for both was the front bumper mounted box for carrying the spare wheel; this is often found on the Berlin version as a preferable alternative or in addition to the collapsible spare wheel, which featured with this model. Electric hook-up was standard and the tent awning now featured a storm-sheet over the open frame and canvas roof.

The Berlin and Helsinki were Westfalia s most well-appointed and luxurious conversions to date, and are still highly sought after today for a classic combination of both style and comfort.

The Berlin

This featured a very different interior layout from previous versions, with the cooking and kitchen facilities along one side under the windows opposite the sliding door. Behind the driver s seat was an open storage space for the collapsible spare wheel with a large cupboard for the gas bottle and water tank. On the inside of the door was a wire storage rack. Next to this was a smaller shelved cupboard for pans and cooking utensils. This was

Der Campingwagen „Helsinki". Und seine inneren Werte.

1 Polstersitzbank hinten
3 Polster auf dem Motorraum
4 Polstersitzbank seitlich
5 Eßtisch schwenkbar
10 Waschregal mit Klapptisch
16 Schrank über dem Motorraum

19 Reserveradverkleidung
20 Küchenlehne (Kopfteil)
33 Vorratsschrank mit Spülbecken
34 Kleiderschrank/Gaskocher
35 Zusatztisch im Fahrerhaus

Der Campingwagen „Berlin" Und wie es drinnen aussieht.

1 Zweisitzige Sitzbank hinten
2 Polster auf dem Motorraum
3 Dachstaukasten
4 Kleiderschrank mit 3 Staufächern
5 Isolierturhe (Kühlruhe gegen Aufpreis)

6 Küchenzeile mit Spülbecken, 2flammigen
  Gaskocher, Schubkästen, Wassertanks
7 Reserverad
8 Schwenkbarer Eßtisch, ausklappbar
9 Drehsitz

wardrobe with a door facing into the living area. A closed roof cupboard was also sited at the rear. An upholstered storage box stool gave extra seating, although the most distinctive new feature was the swivelling passenger seat. Both cab seats came with headrests.

The Helsinki

This closely followed previous successful layouts, with a wardrobe behind the driver's seat, attached to which was a flap-up cooker. This hinged across the gangway and attached to the sink unit for use. The sink unit was sited behind the passenger seat and had a drawer and cool box (or optional fridge) under it with a small open-fronted storage unit with flap table on the side. The spare wheel was stored in the rear and the bench seat/bed was full width, with an additional seat/storage unit under the window between the wardrobe and the rear bench seat. A closed roof cupboard was sited at the rear. Another new feature was the inclusion of an extra table for the cab, which was mounted against the dash and sat between the driver and passenger.

Both models were available in two-tone or single colour, with interior plaid fabric matched to the external colour. Standard Combinations were:

Dakota Beige:
brown/beige/green/black plaid

Sage Green or Pastel White:
green/yellow/black plaid

Chrome Yellow, Light Orange or Pastel White:
green/orange/yelow/black plaid.

The Mosaik programme was replaced by Baukastensatz camping kits, which still allowed pieces to be bought as packages or individual units. These included the wardrobe/cooker/sink section (as a unit or individually), upholstered stools (open and storage box versions), single and bench seating, roof cabinet, tables, panelling and so on, allowing for two basic layouts – single seat with no wardrobe and cooker, or wardrobe and cooker version.

topped by two drawers. Sited on top of the unit was a two-burner cooker and sink with an electric pump tap. The sink and cooker had flap-up tops that doubled as worktops when folded down. The swivel table was

mounted at the end of this unit towards the rear. At the side of the unit, still under the window, was a chest cool box (or optional fridge) and a storage unit. At the rear, in the above-engine compartment, was the

The Helsinki sink/cool box and
wardrobe layout.

The full width bench seat/bed.

L-shaped seating around the table.

A 1978 Helsinki in Sage Green.

Rear view.

Green plaid interior.

The cooker is sited on the cool box unit side and
flaps up across the gangway for use.

1978 CAMPMOBILES

These followed the Berlin style layout, but with cooker and sink unit now running under the side window behind the driver seat. (Cooker on the Deluxe version only.) The collapsible spare wheel was stored at the end of the unit, directly behind the driver. Next to this was a storage chest and 1.1cu ft cool box. At the rear was a clothes closet and a closed roof cabinet. The table was a swivel table, which had a hinged side leaf. The Deluxe version had a refrigerator in place of the cool box, an upholstered storage/trash bin stool and a swivelling front seat for the passenger. There was also a small table, which fitted in the front cab against the dash between the driver and passenger. This stored behind the passenger seat and was secured with a rubber strap. Electric hook-up was standard, but only the Deluxe version included mains water hook-up facilities, gas cooker and underslung gas tank. (Gas equipment was not fitted to vehicles supplied to Canada.) The elevating roof was optional for the basic Campmobile and standard for the Deluxe version.

This layout and options remained during 1976–79, but the versions were now coded as:

P21: standard Campmobile
P22: standard Campmobile
with elevating roof
P27: Deluxe Campmobile.

All were finished in single colours used for specific models; for example, in 1976 P21s were finished in Pastel White, P22s were Chrome Yellow and P27s were Sage Green. Upholstery was finished in either orange/green/yellow or green/yellow check plaid.

From 1976 it was also possible to have air-conditioning installed, with the unit mounted in the the cab roof.

VW Canada Campmobiles mirrored the US versions, except that the swivel seat was standard for all versions. Standard and elevating roof Campmobiles were designated P21 and P22 respectively, but the Deluxe was designated P31. There was no extra leaf for the dining table with these models.

WESTFALIA ID CODES

For 1970–79 model interiors the first number of the Westfalia serial number is the model year; for example: interior number 3.65489 is actually from 1973. Older versions have the build year stamped in. The Westfalia ID plate fixed on the bench seat normally carries the 'SO' number, but in some cases (especially US Buses) it simply reads 'Campmobile 70'. In these cases the interior is named on the M plate as a 'P' code (confusingly when the ID plate says 'SO-73/5', for example, then nothing is mentioned about the interior on the M plate).

P codes are:

P21: Campmobile without pop-up roof, with folding spare tyre
P22: Campmobile with pop-up roof, with folding spare tyre
P23: Campmobile with pop-up roof
P24: Campmobile with pop-up roof and combined gas/electric refrigerator
P25: Campmobile with pop-up roof
P26: Campmobile with pop-up roof and combined gas/electric refrigerator
P27: Campmobile deluxe with pop-up roof, folding spare tyre, combined gas/electric refrigerator (1976–79)
P28: with additional tent for P21 to P27
P29: with additional electricity 220V mains hook-up inlet (for P25 and P26)
P30: 1971–73: Westfalia interior (without pop-up roof)
P30: 1976–79: combined gas/electric refrigerator, with gas cooker unit, side bench in driving direction for storing gas bottles for P21 and P22.
P31: Westfalia with pop-up roof (Canada).
P32: Additional tent for interior P31.

1979–2003: THE T3 (T25) AND T4

The Joker

Westfalia's tradition of design excellence and superb build quality continued into the new T25 range, when they introduced one of their most popular conversions ever – the Joker. It was introduced in 1979 in two versions, Joker 1 (four-seater) and Joker 2 (five-seater with full width rear bench seat). In designing the Joker, Westfalia took full advantage of their

years of experience as leaders in the field of camping interiors, layouts and specifications, and combined this with new materials and the modern refinements now demanded by a more sophisticated generation of VW Camper buyers.

Cabinet work was in light teak laminate wood, with brown plastic trim for all edges including cupboard doors. Upholstery was finished using a modern banded stripe design on a dark or light brown base. There were two tables in the Joker 1; the main dining table was swivel-mounted and stored above the under-window storage units for bedding when not in use. A small swivel table was also mounted at the front for use with the swivelling front seats. Joker 2 had a single table and extra single side seat

This 1979 Joker, owned by George Deverick, was one of the first of the new range, designated Joker 2 with the full width rear seat.

under the window instead of storage cupboards. Another storage cupboard behind the front passenger seat had a flap-down jump seat. The twin hob, sink and fridge were sited behind the driver under the windows. Joker 1 also had a hanging wardrobe at the rear of the units under the window by the end of the bench seat. There was a large storage cupboard in the rear on the same side, and a roof locker on both models. An elevating roof was standard (although a fixed roof option could be specified), and there was an extra double bed in the roof area. The roof was similar in design to that introduced in the early seventies, hinged up at the front, with an integral over-cab roof rack/carry space. Gas and water tanks were slung under the chassis.

By 1980 three roof options were available: the usual Westfalia hinged roof; a higher profile elevating version using the same design principle; and a fixed high roof with a window looking out from the front and two roof lights.

The Joker was very popular and by 1983 was available in several different packages. As well as the Joker 1 and Joker 3, there was the Club Joker (the five-seater with the full width rear seat version) and the Sport Joker, which was the basic weekender model with double bed and table. By now, the teak laminate had been replaced with light grey laminate with dark grey trim to reflect a more modern look.

The last Joker models were produced in 1987 and, for 1988, Westfalia renamed the models California and Atlantic. These still retained the basic Joker layout, but the finish was more luxurious and contemporary in use of materials and colour.

The Joker was still known as the VW Campmobile in North America. It was essentially the same as the European version, apart from US market requirements. Most were designated P23 as the Deluxe model, but, during 1980–81 only, a more basic version, known as the Weekender and designated P22, was marketed in the US, although Westfalia continued to produce the Weekender for the European market.

1982 Brochure.

Der Alltags-Freizeit-Urlaubs-Joker

CLUB JOKER

Der Club Joker – Exclusivität inclusive

1987 brochure.

The contemporary styled cabinet work in pale grey houses the fridge, stainless steel cooker and sink unit.

This 1987 silver edition Club Joker 3 was one of the last of the Jokers to be produced.

Rear headrests were standard.

The Weekender was a no-frills Camper, designed for multi-purpose use. It had a full width rear seat/bed, no cooker or gas supply, and a cool box instead of a fridge, but the space meant that passengers could stretch out in comfort when travelling.

The 1981 Weekender model pictured here is owned by Stan Wohlfarth. As they were only available for a short period in the US they are quite uncommon there. It has a rebuilt 2000cc air-cooled Type 4 style engine with a 914 cam built by Boston Engine from a new block. It has been resprayed twice. Stan has recovered most of the seats with new upholstery and installed new blue vinyl on some of the interior panels (where the original white vinyl material had deteriorated), but the rear corner seat next to the kitchenette still has original upholstery on the two cushions. He added the later model jump seat behind the front passenger seat. Other modifications included cupholders – added throughout the van in colour co-ordinating varieties, a fan above the kitchenette, a brass icebox latch (which does a much better job of keeping the door closed than the original latch), a side step and cab seats with non-adjustable armrests from a 1984 Vanagon. The alloy wheels are aftermarket ones commonly known as Dan Gurney wheels.

1989: T4 CALIFORNIA

The model name California, used for the last T25 conversions, was retained by Westfalia for its new generation based on the T4. The same basic interior layout, proven for the Joker models, was followed, with the cooker, fridge, sink and storage units running under the windows opposite the sliding doors. The interior trim was in wood effect or pale laminate and the packages included many items as standard that were often optional on other conversions.

SPECIAL EDITIONS

Westfalia also marketed limited edition Campers to run alongside their basic spec California conversions. They were only available in left-hand drive and were geared mainly at the European and North American markets. The one shown here is owned by Ralph and June Pettit and is a 2001 special edition called the Generation. These special editions came with many 'extras' as standard, which in this case includes full air-conditioning, heated cab seats, ABS with traction control, twin air bags, cruise control, tinted windows, colour-coded bumpers and mirrors, and on-site diesel central heating. Also included is intelligent remote central locking,

meaning that the sliding door can be operated whilst the others remain locked and the back door can be secured ajar, to give ventilation while remaining secure overnight. The upholstery on the special models was different from the standard models (in this case finished in green and grey), which, although having fewer 'extras', had an almost identical interior.

The Camper shown here features a modular rear seat/bed with two easily removable headrests and two lap and diagonal seat belts. The galley has a two-burner cooker with no grill (a grill is not permitted on German spec vans due to safety regulations). The sink comes with a plastic bowl and a pump to bring water from the 5.5gal (25ltr) onboard and insulated tank. Waste water is drained to a 6gal (27ltr) onboard insulated tank. Both are stored between the furniture and the outer skin, and can be emptied by taps actuated from inside. The fridge uses a low energy system, running solely from the 12V system, and is compressor-operated. Top loading, it looks like a small ice cream fridge, but it is more than a fridge and can operate between –20ºC and +20ºC, so can be both a deep freeze or a hot food store. The leisure battery is a maintenance-free 135amp/hr 'Jelly' battery. Storage is ample with roof and floor cupboards, under-seat and a

wardrobe, as well as handy pouches in the rear. The Gamma radio and cruise control were factory-fitted upgrades.

This is undoubtedly a modern van for a new century, designed for a new generation of owners who demand style, comfort and practicality.

In 2001, to mark fifty years of producing VW Campers, Westfalia introduced a special limited edition version called the California Event, with the distinctive check upholstery. Publicity material even used original Westfalia brochure pictures from the 1950s to pay homage to the origins of the VW Camper, though the luxurious interior bears little resemblance to the old Camping Box interior! A long wheel base, high roof version, the California Exclusive, featured a private bathroom section at the rear, complete with toilet and fold-down sink.

The final special edition was entitled Freestyle, and, although Westfalia continued to produce a limited number of T4 versions after the introduction of the new T5, no T5 versions were ever produced, as in 2004 the agreement between VW and Westfalia came to an end, after fifty-three years of co-operation. Volkswagen did, however, retain the name California for its own version on the T5 platform, which became the first time that VW had actually produced its own version of the Camping wagen.

The 2001 special edition Generation.

157

To many, Westfalia Campers are synonymous with VW Campers, but, contrary to popular belief, there was no such thing as a factory-produced VW Camper, VW preferring to contract camping conversion work to established firms like Westfalia. Campers marketed through the VAG dealerships as Volkswagen Campers were in fact conversions by companies like Westfalia, Devon or Danbury but carrying the benefit of the full VW warranty. For years, VW had always provided the Westfalia Werks with advance information about production changes, even making prototypes available for the Westfalia design team to work with, ahead of production. But when Westfalia was taken over by the Daimler/Chrysler/Mercedes-Benz group, VW was not about to give a rival the details of their new model, the T5! When Volkswagen finally ceased its relationship with Westfalia in 2004, it recognized the need to produce a camping version and so the new T5 range includes a camping version, designated the California. This is fitted out by Volkswagen at the Werks and has also broken with tradition by taking a modern, minimalist design approach. When *Which Motorcaravan*, in November 2004, tested the VW California against the T5 conversions produced by Reimo, Bilbo, Auto-Sleeper and Devon, they declared that whilst many buyers may be put off by, the left-hand drive (no RHD versions), the relatively high price, and the lack of a grill, in their view, if you do most of your motoring abroad this is a real dream machine with some of the most innovative design touches we've seen in a VW Camper. Two models are available, the California Trendline and the slightly higher spec Comfortline, both of which feature an aluminium electro-hydraulically operated elevating roof. In response to UK demands, RHD models were introduced in 2005.

The images here are from Deepcar Motorhomes International of Sheffield. They can be contacted on 0114 288 2660 and are happy to arrange a demonstration of the first factory-produced Volkswagen Camper.

The front seats swivel for dinette style seating. The cooker, sink and cool box are under the side windows.

Clean, modern styling carries through to the hob/sink unit.

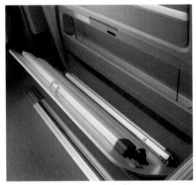

The supplied folding chairs are stored in the tailgate.

The table folds away into a compartment in the sliding door.

Panel Van, Kombi

March 1950–February 1953
Pearl Grey
Dove Blue
Medium Grey
Chestnut Brown
Brown Beige

March 1953–July 1958
Pearl Grey
Grey
Dove Blue
Ivory

August 1958–August 1961
Dove Blue
Ivory
Light Grey
Sealing Wax Red

September 1961–July 1963
Dove Blue
Ivory
Light Grey
Pearl White
Turquoise
Ruby Red

August 1963–July 1964
Dove Blue
Ivory
Light Grey
Pearl White
Turquoise
Ruby Red

August 1964–July 1967
Dove Blue
Pearl White
Light Grey
Velvet Green
Ivory

Microbus and Deluxe

1950–1955

Upper Body Colour	Lower Body Colour
Brown Beige	Light Beige
Stone Grey	Stone Grey
Chestnut Brown	Sealing Wax Red

March 1955–July 1958

Upper Body Colour	Lower Body Colour
Palm Green	Sand Green
Sand Grey	Sand Grey
Chestnut Brown	Sealing Wax Red

August 1958–February 1961

Upper Body Colour	Lower Body Colour
Seagull Grey	Mango Green
Pearl Grey	Pearl Grey
Beige Grey	Sealing Wax Red

March 1961–July 1964

Upper Body Colour	Lower Body Colour
Blue White	Turquoise
Pearl White	Mouse Grey
Beige Grey	Sealing Wax Red

August 1964–July 1965

Upper Body Colour	Lower Body Colour
Blue White	Sea Blue
Blue White	Velvet Green
Beige Grey	Sealing Wax Red

August 1965–July 1967

Upper Body Colour	Lower Body Colour
Cumulus White	Sea Blue
Pearl White	Velvet Green
Beige Grey	Titian Red
Lotus White	Lotus White

L Codes

L21	Pearl Grey	Perlgrau
L22	Medium Grey	Mittelgrau
L23	Silver Grey	Silbergrau
L28	Grey	Grau
L31	Dove Blue	Taubenblau
L37	Mid Blue	Mittelblau
L41	Black	Schwarz
L53	Sealing Wax Red	Siegellackrot
L59	Cherry Red	Kirschrot
L62	Ivory White	Elfenbein (>64)
L63	Post Office Yellow	Postgelb
L70	Grey Silver	Grausilber (>66)
L73	Chestnut Brown	Kastanienbraun
L75	Light Beige	Hellbeige
L76	Brown Beige	Braunbeige
L80	Grey White	Weiss-grau
L82	Silver White	Silberweiss
L84	White	Weiss
L221	Stone Grey	Steingrau
L249	Dove Grey	Taubengrau
L260	Sand Grey	Sandgrau
L282	Lotus White	Lotosweiss
L289	Blue White	Blauweiss
L311	Sand Green	Sandgrün
L312	Palm Green	Palmgrün
L325	Mouse Grey	Mausgrau
L345	Light Grey	Lichtgrau
L346	Mango Green	Mangogrün
L347	Seagull Grey	Möwengrau
L360	Sea Blue	Seeblau
L380	Turquoise	Türkis
L456	Ruby Red	Rubin
L466	Silver Beige	Silberbeige
L471	Stone Beige	Steinbeige
L472	Beige Grey	Beigegrau
L512	Velvet Green	Samtgrün
L528	Grey	Grau
L555	Titian Red	Tizianrot
L567	Ivory White	Elfenbein
L680	Cumulus White	Kumulusweis
L693	Grey Silver	Grausilber

L Code	Model Years	German	English	Roof Colour Abbreviation
L555	1968	Tizianrot	Titian Red	ww
L282	1968–70	Lotosweiß	Lotus White	
L512	1968–70	Samtgrün	Velvet Green	
L620	1968–70	Savannenbeige	Savanna Beige	ww
L87	1968–70	Perlweiß	Pearl White	
L30H	1969–70	Montanarot	Montana Red	ww
L50H	1969–70	Brillantblau	Brilliant Blue	ww
L610	1969–70	Deltagrün	Delta Green	ww
L11H	1971–72	Sierragelb	Sierra Yellow	pw, bl
L31H	1971–72	Chiantirot	Chianti Red	pw, bl
L53D	1971–72	Niagarablau	Niagara Blue	pw, bl
L60D	1971–72	Ulmengrün	Elm Green	pw, bl
L91D	1971–72	Kansasbeige	Kansas Beige	pw, bl
L13H	1973–74	Ceylonbeige	Ceylon Beige	pw
L30B	1973–75	Kasanrot	Kasan Red	pw
L53H	1973–75	Orientblau	Orient Blue	pw
L61B	1973–75	Sumatragrün	Sumatra Green	pw
L20B	1973–79	Leuchtorange	Brilliant Orange	pw
L62H	1974	Baligelb	Bali Yellow	
L65K	1974	Ravennagrün	Ravenna Green	
L20A	1976–77	Marinogelb	Chrome Yellow	pw
			(until chassis no. 2172 079 871)	
L31A	1976–79	Senegalrot	Senegal Red	pw
L57H	1976–79	Ozeanicblau	Reef Blue	pw
L63H	1976–79	Taigagrün	Sage Green	pw, mb
L21H	1977–79	Marinogelb	Chrome Yellow	
			(chassis no. 2172 079 872 and up)	

L Code	Model Years	German	English	Roof Colour Abbreviation
L86Z	1977–79	Agatabraun	Agate Brown	pw, aw, db, mb
L13A	1978	Dakotabeige	Dakota Beige	
LH8A	1978	Dattelbraun	Date Brown	fr
L97A	1978–79	Silbermetallic	Silver Metallic	
L12A	1979	Panamabraun	Panama Brown	mb
LE1M	1979	Mexicobeige	Mexico Beige	
–	all	Grundiert	Prime Red	
L345	all	Lichtgrau	Light Grey	
L50K	all	Neptunblau	Neptune Blue	ww
L567	all	Elfenbein	Ivory	
L90D	all	Pastellweiß	Pastel White	bl

ROOF COLOURS

L Code	Model Years	German	English	Abbreviation
L581	1968–70	Wolkenweiß	Cloud White	ww
L41	1971	Schwarz	Black	bl
L90D	1971–79	Pastellweiß	Pastel White	pw
L91Z	1977	Atlasweiß	Atlas White	aw
L13A	1978	Dakotabeige	Dakota Beige	db
LH3A	1978	Fuchsrot	Fox Red	fr
LE1M	1979	Mexicobeige	Mexico Beige	mb

Note
1968–70– roof and rain gutter painted in upper colour.
1971–79 – roof and body from swage line painted in upper colour.

index